Jas. Wm. Carling

Scientific and Poetical Works of the Last of the Hereditary Bards and Skalas

Jas. Wm. Carling

Scientific and Poetical Works of the Last of the Hereditary Bards and Skalas

ISBN/EAN: 9783337328863

Printed in Europe, USA, Canada, Australia, Japan

Cover: Foto ©Thomas Meinert / pixelio.de

More available books at **www.hansebooks.com**

AND

POETICAL· WORKS

OF THE

Last of the Hereditary Bards and Skalds.

CHICAGO:

THE J. M. W. JONES STATIONERY AND PRINTING COMPANY.

1884.

Mathematic of the Pure and Real.

1881.

Force, or Potential Motion.

Force is pure matter, devoid of everything save extension and elasticity. Force is therefore pure space, a penetrable void, in fact a nothing to the general sense.

Why Force is a Void.

Force is a void because it is weightless, viewless, and intangible. It is pure matter, and being pure, does not possess the qualities of the material save in the possession of its first attributes, penetrability and extension. Force is *expressed* by weight, color and tangibility; but these are only its *expressions*. It *gives* weight, color, and tangibility to matter, yet, in the bestowal, it robs itself of these qualities and sits, "the power behind the throne." Nobody has ever presented us with a lump of pure force, or told us whether its color was Dutch pink or bottle green. As force is not to be found in visible matter it must be sought for elsewhere. Force must be one of two things; it must be either what is commonly called matter, or it must not. There is no way to elude this question; it is either tangible or it is not tangible. If matter, uncaused, can move itself, then there is no such thing as force; but if what we commonly call matter *cannot* move itself, then something *not* material must be the potential power within. Hence, it follows that force is not common matter, and the only thing that remains after the abolition of such material, is a void.

Note.—The writer often uses penetrability and elasticity as synonymous.

Qualities of Force.

Some forces are more refined than others. Everything in the universe is comparative. The lower forces are material by comparison with the higher. Everything in itself, is penetrable and elastic—but only to a higher force; the lower cannot penetrate the higher. The lowest force is common matter, the highest force is thought or mind. All forces are one in the abstract. What we call forces are only its forms.

Expressions of Force.

Everything that distends, boils, bubbles, reports, sucks, flames, attracts or decays, expresses the presence of pervasive force in action. A void without any apparent aid from the exterior universe, will suck in or reject the pressure of its surrounding. What is it that swells a bar of iron, or agitates to the bubbling point the water of a heated kettle? Surely it is not the addition of perceptible material, or we would behold its remains after the agitation had ceased. If the water in boiling weighed *more*, we might imagine that a crowd of unseen elfins were jigging their glee in the rattling pot, disappearing in time for the poor man's meal. Such, I imagine, is not the case—in fact the water, by motion, is actually lighter. Go weigh your pot and find the secret of force !

Form of Motion.

Motion has no other form than that of extension. Without extension, motion exists, but it exists without manifestation. Blot out everything in the universe, and *pure* motion exists. *Pure motion is pure thought.*

Condition of Motion's Manifest Existence.

While *perfect* motion can, and does, exist in the universe without any idea of elasticity connected with it, still, motion cannot be made manifest to the lower reason without elasticity being apprehended. Elasticity extended is latent or potential motion. If there is anything in the universe that is more ideal than thought, then thought is elastic to it; if not, then thought is totally inelastic, though acting upon, and through, an elastic medium. At any rate, to the material world, pure thought shall ever be inelastic, since, like pure motion, it possesses no quality known in the universe.*

The Three Phases of Motion.

Motion has three phases—two extremes and a mean. The first is the annihilation of extension or *pure* motion; the second is common matter; the last is extended force. The first is complete contraction, the second is rest, the third is repulsion. They are mind, matter, and force, and are well expressed in the shape of a biangle. The first is infinite contraction, the second is contraction-repulsion, the third is infinite repulsion. The latter, however, never pervades the infinite, since there are limitless oceans of repulsions in the universe, and these reject the sweep of repulsing force and bar its pathway through the profound. Nothing but thought becomes infinite, and it achieves infinitude in the annihilation of extension. But all-extension and no-extension are one, and thought achieves infinity only in the instantaneity of change, *imagined* change.

---

* That is, *in itself* it possesses no one quality but *all*. The all is vulgarly supposed to be the none, as it seems out of comparison, or, infinite. The elastic means the penetrable, above.

Pure Motion.

We must now soar into the iciest and purest domain of mathematical reason in order to comprehend the idea of pure motion. In the first place, *extension is an expression of motion.* Even primeval space without the shiver of a single atom being manifested, entirely devoid of anything approaching the slightest rustle, was in a state of conceivable motion, for it *extended* everywhere. Extension being a form of motion cannot be *pure* motion,* for *something* moves in order to be extended; it may be only an idea expressing itself, but it expresses motion at any rate. *Pure* motion, therefore, lies behind extension— beyond imagination, but not beyond pure thought. We have the capacity to *know* the superior, though we may not comprehend it. Pure thought and pure motion being one, are the conditions through which all motion and thought are manifested. I mean by the word *pure,* the untainted essence of things.

Does Pure Motion Exist?

Pure motion being the annihilation of everything that human mind conceives of below, the question follows, Does pure motion exist? Yes, but like everything else from time to life, only during the instant of its annihilation. *Death and existence are one.*

Impossibility of Touch or Rebound Without the Instantaneous Annihilation of Distance Between.

It is impossible for two things to rebound from each other without a material contact *somewhere.* There may be fluids and ethers innumerable between the opposing bodies, but *something* attenuated finally meets its Greek, and closes to a perfect contact, the result of which being an instantaneous rebound. Pure thought always ensues in a rebound. Two minds may send two stones crashing against each other, but a third mind, *spontaneously created*, sends them staggering backwards again. As extension or distance is annihilated in the contact between two opposing bodies, it follows that pure motion or complete inextension ensues. Thus it always is with motion It began with thought, and is flung backwards by thought. Pure thought is the *final cause* of everything.

Common Motion.

Motion is thought. Common motion is expressed thought ; pure motion is inexpressed thought. I am compelled to repeat myself in order that the reader may *think*, using the ideas I bring nearest to mind. When you imagine extension, *you* move in thought. Extension (or anything else) *will not move for you.* You must *always* move in order to comprehend motion, for you do your *own* thinking.

---

* *Pure* motion is complete rest. A thing that is perfectly pure has no relations with extraneous ideas—it ceases therefore to be manifested. It exists here in the moment of annihilation.

Why Thought is Pure Motion.

That which is pure or perfect becomes its own opposite. *Perfection is annihilation, and the infinite is perfection.* Pure motion is rest; it is only the condition necessary to evolve *actual* motion. Two objects in meeting jar the ether between them, and the immediate result is the annihilation of distance between the opposing rims of ether. Immediately with the annihilation of distance, ensues a resisting motion, formed by the creation of a perfect void or solid (both meaning the same thing) at the moment of clash—this solid-void is an *idea disk* created by the spontaneous generation of a motion. It is the smallest evolution in the universe, and is the form taken on by pure thought *in manifesting itself to the sensible world.* Pure thought is pure motion or inextension, because nothing that we conceive *of* is thought. In order to know *of* a thing, we must first *not be* the thing in question. Had we never gone to sleep we should never have known the existence of thought. Vice versa: What we see, and the act of seeing, are two different things. Pure thought is the complete negation of everything save the infinite; hence it comprehends all but the infinite. Were it more than infinite it could comprehend the infinite. Pure thought is above annihilation, for it *is* annihilation; it can annihilate everything but itself. Nothing can act upon itself; the superior must act upon the inferior; hence thought is above the law of decay—such as is known in the inferior universe.* In *reality* there is no such thing as decay; rot is only *change.*

As inextension is the cause of a rebound, it follows that motions are all caused by a rebound from *somewhere.* A motion *to* a thing is nothing but a rebound *from* a thing.

The Idea of Space and Time.

Without the possession of thought, there is no idea of space and time. Space and time to us, depend upon thought. Why may not the expression of space and time, in objective nature, also depend upon thought? If nature does not express space and time, we are the creators of our own universe, and the objective world is a delusion; if nature *does* express space and time, then nature is founded upon thought as well as our reason. We are only nature comprehending itself, and we, at least, owe our entire self-recognition and existence to thought.

Reality of the Objective.

There is proof, however, that nature exists as well as we. Were the universe a myth and the creation of fantasy, our desires could receive no check or limit. As it is, however, we are bounded and abridged and compelled to get out of the way of other ideas. That we are compelled to believe in our own creations is farcical, since by doubting them all with genuine honesty we could overcome the com-

---

*I may use *pure* thought and *common* thought without the adjective; the reader will easily discriminate between.

pulsion, or positively know that some outside influence was at work.*
In fact, we do not exist at all (the outside world furnishing us with every
picture and sensation), save for one stubborn fact—*we think.*

Reality of the Ideal.

There is no difference between the real and ideal, save that one is
denser than the other. The *perpetuity* and *densification* of the ideal is
the real.

Does Time Exist?

Time either does or does not exist. If time is changeless, it does
not exist; if it is progressive and changeful, it does exist. Time has been
called duration. Duration of what? Of space? Time *is* space, per-
vading it and making it subject to ideal conditions. If space and time
were always the same, then nothing has been evolved—the universe is a
thwarted and insulted waste. But time does exist, all-enduring and
ever-changing, the parent of actual motion. Time as a *whole* does not
change, thus showing the ideality of its succession.

Why Time is Motion.†

Because it conveys the idea of succession.
Because it extends, and is now extending.
Because it is the synonym of change.
Because its past exists in the present and thickens the idea of
motion in the universe.
Because without the *present* existence of the past, the *now* has
nothing to sustain it.
Because its *perpetuity* and *densification* have terminated in *actual
motion!*

Why Space and Time are one under a Duality of Form.

Space and time are a hermaphrodite one, male and female, negative and positive. Abolish time, and space endures; abolish space, and
you have pure motion.

Why Space is Pure Matter.

Space is pure matter because it is extended. It is a pure solid
because it is a void. It is now, however, an elastic, all-pervading and
drowning ocean of ether, its solidity being destroyed by the simultaneous
being of time or motion.

---

*In dreams we never doubt, for we never reason consecutively. To doubt that we dream is
to be awake. So to doubt of the here is to exist in the hereafter. As by thinking we know of our
existence, so by thinking we know of exterior existence. All is thought, all is real.

†People may say that time is not in reality motion, but only an *idea* of motion that we
have "originated." If the reader will think dispassionately for a time, he will find that all
things are likewise ideas that we have "originated."

Why Pure Void is a Solid when Unchanged by Motion.

Pure void is a solid because it is without parts. Being without parts, it is impenetrable to pressure, as there is no room for an opening. Pure void, unpervaded by motion, is impenetrable to decay. Pure void of itself cannot exist; it cannot contract or expand. It therefore changes.

How Time Acted Upon Space.

Time being simultaneous with space, made it elastic. Elasticity is the first condition of *actual* motion. Time and space lost their individuality for an instant in becoming the elastic. The elastic was one, the perfect blending of time and space. But this elastic did not remain the same. At the instant of its existence a new time was born, and changed it into another elastic. This elastic was ethereal darkness, and with the evolution of time its elasticity became showering.

The True Significance of Time.

Time does not go by the clocks of fools. The true tick of the times lies in men's brains. No mind exists at once in the same space as another. Space is time; therefore are we individual. Time is a condition of change or motion alone. He who is most developed has lived the longest in *actual* time. The grim genius, hoary with an age that almanacs cannot give, stares like a god from his cradle, crowing his warlike delight at the universe—surveying its truth through vast, unpronounceable laws.

Is it Possible to Destroy the Past Motions of Time?

I have *glanced* at this subject in a previous paragraph, but I have space enough at command, and I will cleave through it "with conscience wide as hell." It is not possible to destroy the past motions of time. If the motions of yesterday do not at present exist; if they are entirely abolished, then the motions we perceive around us were made a second ago—in fact the world began to-day, and we were born without fathers and mothers! *Fact is motion.* To deny that every motion which has ever occurred is not in existence up to the present date is to contradict all fact and abolish the reality of the universe.

What We May Know of Matter.

What do we know of matter? Everything. Scientists allow we may know of its qualities, but deny that we know of its essence. Its essence is extension, and that we can measure by a tape line. Our knowledge of matter is based on pure mathematics. The discoveries mentioned within this book place philosophy on a sounder basis than that which physical science can claim.* The latter is founded on mere *appearances*, both empty and metaphysical; the former is founded only on the pure and real.

Does Nothing, Totally Disconnected with any Idea, Exist ?

A complete nothing without some quality adhering to or expressing it does not exist. If there is anything, to be paradoxical, that is a nothing to *everything in the universe*, then it does not exist *in* the universe. There are no two infinites; and thus it contradicts itself. We may call things nothings as figures of speech, but we must remember that, though all extension or space may be abolished, unconditioned thought remains. Unconditioned thought can be *called* nothing till the world *digests* these lines.

The Philosophy of Denial.

The first lesson of the true philosopher is to learn how to apply the lash to his own arguments before he attempts to scourge the ideas of others. In the first place, we will deny that thought is inextension. I mean, of course, inexpressed or pure thought. Now, if we deny that pure thought is inextended, then everything that is extended is thought, *but expresses nothing.** Here we deny the outer universe. Now if we imagine that our thought is likewise extended but is pure, and therefore incapable of comprehending anything save that which is *beneath* extension, we abolish all knowledge of the outer, and, therefore, ourselves. One thing thought must be—extended, inextended or inexistent.

Denial of the Reality of Space as Matter.

Three things only exist, matter, motion and thought. They are in reality one, but we will call them so for convenience. Pure space is its own filling, and this cannot be nothing, for I have proven *absolute* nothing to be inexistent.

Pure space could not stretch any more, for it was stretched to infinity since time began. Neither could it contract any more without losing its purity and oneness. Now we have the idea of space as it would have been had motion never existed—a solid universe, more hard and impenetrable than beaten steel.

---

* The experimentalists at present occupy the eye of the world, *but they have never discovered a single law.* Gravitation was known as a theory before Newton; what has he left it? A theory still. Both evolution and the conservation of energy were ideas known to metaphysicians thousands of years ago. The experimentalists say they have *demonstrated* the law of persistent energy. *They have not.* Motion does not change into heat, for heat *is* motion. The attritional force of a moving ball is caused by the action of that force upon other things ; he force itself leaves *during the ball's motion*, and speeds to its "line of least resistance."

† And why? Because nothing can comprehend itself, and if pure thought was extension it could only comprehend that which has no extension—in other words nothing. Yet a thought in being expressed has extension ; hence we cannot comprehend anything smaller than our idea disks.

Is There More Matter in Existence Than Formerly ?

There is more matter in existence than formerly, more weight, more density.* Time was when space did not weigh a single ton, when its motion was thoroughly ideal and refined. The primeval matter of space has been gathered and centralized in stars—*a different space* smiles on those blazing orbs. The weight of space achieved its maximum point during the period of the great conflagration ; since then the weight of the universe has been *gradually decreasing.*† The universe is returning to its original condition of mind, with this difference however, the mind is *expressed.* Weight is discordance—the enemy of all harmony and refinement. I mean the weightiness of terrestrial things, not the comparative weight of the perceptional and ideal. But nothing really *is* but the ideal.

Cause of Weight.

Weight is caused by the pull and drag of variously opposing suctions. Every rock is composed of illimitable quadrillions of voids or suctions, each forming its own centre of gravity, and acting upon every other void. The space between suctions is the hardness of common matter ; the suctions themselves, the force or forces of common matter. When a rock decays into slime or slush there is a manifest tendency among these voids to centralize towards a common centre, to become more harmonious, and to evolve into vegetal scum. Plants are nothing but woven forces, gently attracted from the air and ground.‡ Gravitation being caused by suction, it is easy to finish the famous theory into a demonstrable law.

The Test of Truth.

From Pontius Pilate down to Herbert Spencer, we have heard the question: What is truth ? Truth is pure thought or motion. Still, as we deal with appearances mostly, the best test of truth is negation. *We are, or we are not; it is, or it is not.* Of one or the other it must be. Perfection as a one *cannot* exist; the infinite is continually annihilating itself.‖

Law of Negation.

All things sprang from their opposites. Virtue sprang from evil, or it would cease to be comparative, and, therefore, not virtue. Cold sprang from immovable heat; heat sprang from motional cold. Light sprang from darkness in motion; darkness existed from light at rest.

---

*This is used in its contracted every-day sense. There is more actual matter now, but not more potential matter—that always *was* boundless. We *see* more matter, but the unseen, the potential, is just as bulky as ever. The more sight we possess, and sight perceives only the ideal, the more matter we behold.

†Apparently decreasing, for what belonged to *masses* is being centralized in *points.*

‡ Man, the ape, and the dog are variations from the bear. Man did not spring from the monkey.

‖ *What is Truth* is satisfactorily answered in " The Dignity of Man."

Fire sprang from frozen gas; water sprang from condensing fire. Hate sprang from love of *something else;* love sprang from hate of something else. Freedom is known by slavery; slavery by freedom.

What Else Does the Law of Negation Prove?

That a thing without a comparative cannot exist. That a one is forced to become a two. That *all things are dual.* That pure truth is unmanifested without form or extension, and that whatever *is,* is real in its sphere.

Why is the One Forced to Become a Two?

A thing must remain without expression and not be, or be, and annihilate itself in the expression. In either case it becomes something else, for by *not being* what it was, it expresses the same as being what it was not. Pure thought is annihilation or creation—both are the same. Pure thought annihilates itself only to express and give form to its being. A thought, in expressing itself, no longer thinks of the future, but of its own present—the past. It surveys its next neighbor with a steady eye, and comprehends that neighbor alone. It needs something succeeding to comprehend itself—so on to the end. Woe be to the unjust when the last thought-void is evolved, and they are confronted by their felon lives. Woe be to the bristling lawyer and the sly politician; the coward robbers of the poor—the lecherous preacher and the pompous miser; fainting with aged craft, hoary in villainy!

Law of Tune.

One-half of all truth is association. Tune is nothing but stringed association. It is the association, and not the stringing, that plays the most on the emotions. We have nothing but stringing now-a-days. Music has grown to be an artistic titillation—we take it into our ears as our fathers took snuff. No pure notes must be allowed any more than raw colors in a painting. A love-song must be as lovers *speak*—soft, plaintive, tender and with varying inflections. A wreck song should be pervaded by wails and vasty dwells a war song by drum-rolls. Short sounds, save in a merry glee, should be avoided—beauty despises abruptness. A poem is a song in monotone. People recite poems, however, as though they were seized with the colic—jerks have become the rule. The schoolmasters should remember that they are not poets, and that *their* method is not the poets' method. Books will not make a bard.

Presence of Design.

That there is what is called design in the universe is proven by the fact that we not only conceive of it, but in a measure possess it. If we, who are but nature comprehending itself, possess it, so do the lesser creations possess it in a *simpler* form. The law of gravitation is design. So is every other law. We cannot will without designing ; a stone cannot fall without a cause. *When causes cease to act* we will talk of chance, till then let us expend our forces on other subjects.

The Origination of Change in Space.

Space being infinite was as one. A thing of one cannot exist. A thing or fact must have two sides, or it has no side. Perfection is annihilation, and one is perfection. Pure space is pure void. Pure void is solid. Pure void is the annihilation of space, for it *solidifies* it. *The* pure solid was infinite, and having no opposite or comparative it annihilated itself. Neither void nor solid could exist alone. They became a two, and space existed perennially as an elastic or penetrable void.

How did the universal solid become weightless simultaneously with its being ? *Because every portion of it bore the same amount of pressure* and where *everything* supported itself, *nothing was supported.* A void the size of a needle point would have given weight to the universe, but such a void never was, or could be created, without an agency, and that agency had never existed until Jewry saw wonders!

Cause.

The first cause of *everything*, as I said before, is pure thought. The second cause of everything is an elastic void. As pure thought is unserviceable and incomprehensible, to find out the causes of things it would be best to use void as first cause, since it is the expression or *comprehensible* form of pure thought.

How to Get the Exact Causes of Every Substance or Quality.

The way in which to get the causes of things is to enumerate every quality they possess and then mark down the opposites of these qualities. Thus gravitation gives weight, color, and tangibility to matter ; its cause must therefore lie in that which is weightless, viewless, and intangible. Of course a void is the cause. *Force and cause are one* under different names. Force is a void and attracts matter to its centre ; cause is a void and repulses force from its center. We are juggled with by too many terms.

How the Individual Sprang from the Whole.

Space as a *complete whole* had no extension. It was one boundless, transparent immensity, completely harmonious, and devoid of atoms or parts. It was pure darkness and thought, a blank eternity, without a voice or an expression within. The one was annihilated by the all. *Every portion of it* being without extension, tried to express itself in extension ; but as *everywhere* tried to express itself at the same time, nothing but a *universal* change ensued. This occurred (ideally) twice, and evolved the elastic from the solid and void. But in the third motion, the annihilation of the elastic, a faint idea of inharmony occurred. The elastic could neither be annihilated back again to the solid and void, without annihilating the time and motion that gave it being, nor could it annihilate itself forwards, without evolving two elasticities into being. This it simultaneously did, evolving matter and force into existence. The number three is the symbol of differentiation in all things. It corresponds to gray in color, *me* in tune, the hermaphrodite in sex, reproduction-decay in life, differentiation in number, and centralization in form. As it is the symbol of all progression, so it is, through opposition, the symbol of decay.

What is Decay?

Decay is but another term for motion. Nothing can change in itself without decay. Decay is life; we cannot evolve the new without dying. *No fire ever started in the universe without a decay;* something must be destroyed or sundered from its centres before a flame appears. Flame is but the disruption of the minute; *everything is afire if spread outwards and refined.* Smoke is unignited flame before its particles form into smoke, they pass muster under the form of wood, coal, oil, iron—perhaps an old cobbler's boot. There was a time *when the gas was not on fire.* What was it before? And before that—and before?* These questions must be answered by stormier minds than the laboratory furnishes—stormers of truth's most fearful fortresses, warriors of song, men of tempestuous hearts and swelling souls. Science needs its "forlorn hope" to scale its precipitous ramparts, mounting on the whirlwind, and plundering in the clouds—there do I behold the forms of the future's bards. None but the poets are the true scientists ; all else but barren numbskulls and not to the manner born.

The Pre-nebular Creation.

In the beginning there was neither goodness nor design; a godless darkness reigned alone. Nothing was before but the primeval night, slumbering and silent in a boundless void—a frozen universe of dreary and unutterable horror.

Eternities went drowsily onwards, yet nothing came—time itself appeared to swoon into a death of inanition and torpor.

Yet in that voiceless waste lay creations uncreated; in its fearful abyss lay the futurities of woman and man—of woman the beautiful, and man the brave—the sweetness of kindness, the fervor of loving; the stormful earnestness and torrid power.

The first law forced into existence amidst these endless solitudes was the law of being or decay. Decay is reproduction, and nothing is originated without a death. Darkness was a condition; all conditions have reality, and no condition is eternal. *The darkness decayed, its decay fell, and thus established the eternity of motion.* On all sides it decayed; raining for illimitable centuries ; above, below, before and behind. Space trembled in its tiny delirium ; at first abstract and invisible, then humming and fearful—bridging eternity till man re-echoed

---

*The reader will bear in mind that *time is decay*, that *all* change in masses is decay, that motion *cannot be* without the "annihilation" of space, showing that the *idea* as well as the *reality* of change is decay.

greedy in war. Wherever this motion was greatest, wherever there was but as much as a point in excess, there was the greatest attraction in the universe; and towards that centre all things turned.

Amidst the depths wandered an unending thunder, faintly bellowing through far-fading boundaries, muttering the long roll of eternity through the ceaseless infinitude.

The gases formed in dark duality, evolved, singing a windy song to the march of time. And now thickened the great nebulæ, brewed from the boundless; thicker and thicker, until space was dense as a drowning ocean—falling to the centre, as sound rose high and chaos roared.

All darkness bounded, urged by tremendous vacuums, the filling of which thrashed the storm-clouds into hurricanes, and whirled through its hurryings with tempestuous power. Lightnings appeared, drizzling from the rifts, illuminating at intervals the frigid down-pour; but their fearful powers were quickly smothered by the weight of eternity pressing them centrewards—on, on on; to the boundaries of the unknown. Let there be light! Let there be light! Let there be light! And the immeasurable wastes, blown into straightened lines, thundered into heat with tumultuous speed, evolving the highest decay of immensity's sundering motions.

Thus did creation dawn; thus did the visible evolve from the invisible; thus did the beginning grow dense from the perpetual; and the sublimities dream through a chaos burning—from a dull red universe of awakening fire.

Creation of the Universal Systems.

Space raved for thousands of years, a wilderness of flames and glare, closing in on all sides with a fury whose uncontrollable rift and shock the ruggedest mind is unable to conceive. None have ever gazed upon it—and only That which has beheld the red original can tell. All the powers that had existence lent their most terrific aid to swell the rage of its unimaginable destruction, tumbling in precipitous mountains of fire through oceans and hells of never-ending ruin. All space heaved onwards, bounding in cataracts of flame, crashing like earthquakes upon billows of explosion, leaving behind it but mightier thunder-seas that rocked with conflagration, dinning the boundless in one long, horrid and interminable roar.

The densest part of this molten universe withered itself up to blackness from its very intensity, and left a gravitating *centre of cold* in the midst of the burning universe.

Against this cavernous centre all space warred, eager to crush it by the pressure of external matter. The void gave way and the flames roared in victorious joy. It was pressed to the point of annihilation, and a rebound ensued. The fires went staggering backwards and the void grew. This process was continued for an almost limitless period, until the void, rimmed with fires, had created an outer void, and this an outer void, until the universe-globes surrounding each other, yet separated by inconceivable distances, formed the condition of things at present existing. The universe-globes are formed out of nebulous dust *or stars*. The universe that we surround is invisible, so small does it seem to our conception—our light will perhaps never reach it. The universe without us is also invisible, so terrific and appalling is the distance between. All the universes within contract and expand (as if they were breathing) to the growth and pressure of the universes without.

The Sun's Fearful Leap.

On the borders of the great nebulous universe without us, old Sol, in attempting to fill in a rift or sun-spot (for the universes are nothing but star-suns), wriggled and fell. Its tiny, nebulous mass had taken a leap into the dark—towards the inner universe, invisibly attracting. Sol was then a comet with a huge tail. He ran on for trillions of years, until he neared the surface of the inner star-sun. Here he was beaten back, tail foremost, and ran outwards towards his parental nebulæ. But its heat-whirr rejected him again, and he ran headlong onwards on the same old journey. He flew back and forth for illimitable ages, until his period, shortened by the growth of stars, and being reduced to a mere stroke in orbital motion, his scarce-restrained violence caused him to *swirl round*, at which point he evolved his planets and moved in a circular "line of least resistance." Halfway between Hercules and Canis Major lies the inner universe. It can be pointed at through stellar gravitation.

All universes create man—all, all, all. Man is an astronomical animal; he is created like suns and planets. Man is not the creature of chance ; he is the destiny of all creation. These inner universes have furnished their Shakespeares before a single orb in this universe was formed.

We are less than the dirt they tread upon ; our best are but Laurentian wrigglers in the presence of that ancient and sublimated civilization.

Arcturus blazed ere the sun was born, and the Dog Star danced ere the world was new, but we are the latest of all ; our system scarcely cooled ; thinking ourselves high, we are with the lowest in all the universes !

NOTE.—The writer *believes* that the so-called velocity of light is nothing but the *speed of the sun* flying through space. It is as yet only a guess ; time will prove its falsity or truth.

Centripetal and Circular Motion.

When the centripetal can no farther go it changes into a circular motion. When the circular can no farther go it changes into the centripetal. Thus light eventually slopes off from its centre with a cometary crook of bluish-looking ether. All suns were and *are* comets.

Heat and Cold.

All cold is contraction ; all heat expansion. All diseases spring from either too much heat or too much cold. There is nothing (omitting accidents) in disease but *fever* and *chill*. The *only* cure lies in suppressing or exalting the temperature.

What are Memories ?

Memories are reflections coupled with the power of *beholding*. Everything that reflects an image expresses a memory ; but everything cannot *behold* its own reflections. It needs a multitude of inner reflections, verging in refinement and size up to the purity and inextension of pure thought to comprehend the form, size, color, and brilliancy of the outer universe.

Theories or Facts ?

Some may imagine that the author of these lines is a speculator and a metaphysician. He is a mathematician ; a strict deducer from empirical facts ; from laws that have been *demonstrably* proved. That he has grasped them as one, and evolved forth newer truths from the mass does not necessarily infer that new truths are not equally as good as old ones. To prove, however, that they are only abstract to those wits who have no bigger souls than flies, and that they are not spun from the inner consciousness as a spider spins his web, he will, after this book is published, prove every fact and law by *physical demonstration*.

What Is Consciousness?

Consciousness is a perception of space. Nothing can perceive its real self, hence consciousness is not space. Consciousness is below sensation—it is the bridge between what is commonly called mind and matter. I refer to pure consciousness; that which is simply *aware;* but aware of nothing but space. Vegetation is in a state of consciousness and sensation. I mean according to the writer's definition below.

Sensation.

*Sensation is perception of motion.** A thing possessing sensation cannot understand sensation until it possesses volition and emotion; for without the higher it cannot comprehend its lower perceptions. Sensation appears to consciousness as a black surrounding—but it does not even know that it is black. Structural destiny and education determine whether the consciousness shall evolve to a higher condition.

Volition.

Volition with sensation, appears still black to consciousness. A confused idea of space pervades; a notion of nothingness. The will cannot act, for volition cannot comprehend itself. Heat and cold are dimly felt. Consciousness shrinks *involuntarily* to touch or chill. There is no self-motion. Some flowers may be in this state of existence.

---

*Perception of motion is here meant for perception of extension. The lowest sensation and consciousness are one.

Emotion.

Motion is strongly felt. The blackness appears to whirr. Dots of light appear under severe shock. Self-motion faintly manifested. Pain comprehended. No idea of joy save that afforded by touch. Emotion not felt.

Perception.

Emotion faintly felt. The senses perfected. Dawn of desire. Light perceived of a grayish, almost colorless, transparent hue. Figures perceived as dark shadows, without form or idea of distance, in fore-ground.

Intelligence.

Capacity for receiving great quantities of light manifested. Color and form perfected through education. Revenge, love and all the emotions fiercely active. Pictures of the outer world, more or less correct, appear in the field of vision.

Manifestations of Consciousness, or as It Appears to the Mental View.

Consciousness being evolved through the jarring contact of oppos-ing voids (for there is an interval of eternity between common matter), it follows that in rebounding, if not stopped by something almost as powerful as itself, something prepared by nature to arrest its expansion, it will dissipate itself through space as common energy, and so lose its individuality in the realm of mind.* If, however, it is surrounded by the voids of intelligence, perception, emotion and sensation, its rebound is arrested, and it is compelled by an iron fate to manifest itself as the "I" of Toby the dog, or Tommy the fool. The higher mind-voids are situated next to consciousness, the commoner mind-voids are more to the outwards.

Sleep.

By closing the eyes and dulling the attention we sleep. Sleep is nothing but the closing of the sense-avenues of the front and side-head, leaving the back-head passages faintly open. When we close our eyes, nostrils, mouths and ears, we are literally *dead* in every department save that which relates to the reproductive—we reproduce food for both the physical and mental. The former if used becomes the imaginative; in dreams we often exhaust to a great extent the mental supply. When asleep our consciousness, in using this supply, having nothing to attract its attention, reflects the pictures of other memories, often confusedly; hence, we dream.

*The writer has discovered since writing the above that nothing is dissipated, that *every-thing* is conserved, and that nothing *eventually* can be rejected save by the passive permission of one will to the excited demands of another.

Reproduction in its Relation to the Memories.

Everything in the universe is reproduced by contraction and repulsion, by pressure and rejection. So with the memories. Man is female to the universe; every sense-avenue is a receptive sexual organism. The eyes, the mouth and ears are but *modifications* of the reproductive sexual system of man—to understand one of these organisms *thoroughly* is to understand all. Man is brave enough in body; *mental courage and daring* are almost unknown. Had I the forming of a young man's mind, I would continually impress upon him the fact that he was juggled with and be-fooled by nature; that most of his imaginings were lies, and that he must contradict every impression until he is aware of the secret realities of things. I would not cry that "the sun is warm" until I had penetrated the soul of heat. I would not be fluttered by love itself, until I had found out the "*reason why.*"

Does Sensation Exist in the Memories?

Sensation exists in the memories. I can tell the taste of an apple in the dark. Had I not remembered it I would not have known it from a door-knob. We cannot recollect memories of sensation, however, as well as we do of thought, for thought is only a reflection from feeling, and in reflecting the feelings of the past, we only get thought. Hence the memories of sensation are past thoughts acting on the organization of the present.*

Individuality of Mind and its Memories.

No two minds, or memories, can exist in the same space and time. The memory of yesterday is not the memory of to-day. Were the memories not separated in a measure by time and space, we would remember everything. Having space and time, they possess locality; hence one train of ideas will rediscover another. It is from "losing the way" that we forget the past. Tell me what occurred in every detail six years ago, and I will tell you exactly what happened seven or five years ago. Memory is effect; pure thought is cause.

Abolition of Cause Into Effect, and Vice Versa.

Pure thought abolishes itself into expressive memory. A memory-void *express* volition, sensation, etc., etc., but does not feel or move of its own accord. Nothing but a higher thought or shock can make memories ex-comprehensible, and this shock occurs with the cessation of earthly consciousness. Death is but another name for shock. It is the thought, the "baby cry" of a new existence.

* As *all* sensations combine into thoughts, it behooves the scientist to know that sensation is unknown after death. Nothing but intellectual sensation (or inspiration) rules. Hence, only the inspired poets can *feel* beyond this world. The strongest *hater* is the greatest of living men, since he is the greatest *lover*.

How the Minds Act on Each Other.

Perception communicates to intelligence, emotion communicates to perception, volition communicates to emotion, sensation communicates to volition, and the outer universe communicates to sensation. When the mind wishes to communicate with the outer universe, the higher descends to the lower.

How We Move Our Hands and Feet.

The higher minds charge the lower with force, making that part which does not need to be moved entirely negative, while the part that is to be moved is shocked and flung violently to the point desired. The motions of the arms are in a measure involuntary ; habit acquired in infancy, makes careful effort almost automatic, eventually.

Can Mind Penetrate Stone Walls?

If sound can penetrate stone walls, if light can enter through the straight and comparatively harmonious pores of glass, so can mind roam at will through iron doors, and enter mountains of granite as easily and gracefully as a bird flies through the ether. Not only are its particles refined far beyond light, but they possess a penetrability that laughs at every obstacle known to the inferior universe, when under the influence of will.

How Matter Begins to Know Itself.

A void is first necessary. Its centre is shocked. The void is now *aware*. The shock creates a smaller centre. This is shocked. The void is now *aware of the aware.* This creates a still smaller centre, which, on being shocked, creates a smaller ; and so on, until the void *knows.*

Man's Individuality Nothing but Memory.

Some bread-and-butter milksop who loves his flesh better than his mind, will whine over the fact that nothing but memory is immortal. But let him absorb this fact into his bacon mind. The memory of the flesh is the *reality* of the flesh ; for the flesh is being constantly absorbed into memory of the flesh. We are nothing but memory. Abolish the memory and, save for the few pounds of fool we leave behind us, we are totally annihilated.

What Becomes of the Tons of Food We Have Eaten?

So much food means so much force. It cannot mean matter, or our bellies would be bigger. Does all that force lie in the brain ? Could it remain there without explosion ? No.

Does the Force Leave the Body in Exerting Its Strength ?

The force does not leave the arms when the body is pushing an object. If it did there could be no push. If the sensory force left the body we would feel all over ; everything would be disarranged, there would remain no separation or individuality of the channels. The will does not evaporate, but leaves by the brain and in company with thought. When there has been great exertion, with corresponding repulsion of will-force from the mind, the intervals between ideas are greater in proportion to the strain. Every idea is surrounded with will-force, but at this period the surrounding is enormous. The rejection of the will results in poverty of that material, leaving the emotions stunned, and the senses dull and tired.

Loss of Memory.

Memories are never lost. Tell me all of '63, and I shall tell you all of '64. It is only the faculty of recalling them that we lose ; as when the structure is weakened by excesses or disease. The mind has only enough material to evolve its own ideas, without having recourse to the strained attention of memorizing distinctly. There must be forces enough at hand to meet the requirements of concentration—enough of mind-flow to issue what I would call *blank voids.* Without *blank voids* (or thought-atoms) we cannot re-photograph the past.

Law of Reproduction.

The growth of things cease when growth or pressure threatens the annihilation of the internal—then pro-creation or weight-rejection begins. At the stage of self-completion a sun or planet rejects its ring, a flower its leaves, and an animal its spermatoid. With re-production self-decay begins. At twenty-six or thereabouts we appear to grow no more, for the drain of the system caused by the creation of perfect reproductive fluid, is greater, or at least equal to the supply we absorb from food. This process decays with age, and men not only grow fat in age, but, as I am informed, gain an inch or two in height. Of course where decay has gained the ascendancy, as is often the case, people appear to wither and dry up—the fate of man is the fate of the world. A drop of semen is worth over thirty drops of arterial blood. Whether a man is chaste or not this fearful robbery goes on all the same ; its lack of use, potentially a power, gives and bestows no equivalent save in thought or reproduction. Every man through this cause loses from his weight almost a bucket-full of *arterial blood* every week of his existence below!

Sex.

Sex is only another name for form. *Everything is formed by weight and pressure.* As this is a law, it applies to *ideas* as well as to objects. Sexual love by right is *pure*—what is called *impure* is, to the mass unconscious love of reproduction. The brain is the seat of the loves. The back brain is love of the personal or individual; the front is love of the general or universal. The middle and top-brain is the neutral ground between both—the impersonal imperceptible, the moral. In the back-head, love of form becomes love of one form; in the middle head, love of *some* forms (ideality); in the front head, love of all forms. So with every quality in the mind. All *great* minds are high on the top-head near the forehead, with sloping back top-head. Humble and bashful-proud only in their scorn of fools.

Expansion in Relation to the Memories.

Expansion is annihilation, contraction is preservation. This is a law. All things that contract, preserve—salt, cold, etc., etc. All things that expand, destroy—heat, decay, etc., etc. As space expands everywhere, it is the boundless synonym of change, destruction or decay. Contraction is form. Therefore, sex is contraction. Form gives individuality; so does sex or contraction. I could discover an eternity of laws on this subject, and amaze the reader by newer combinations, but I can only suggest here what has been, by the writer, almost carried to its furthermost limits. By furthermost limits I mean the limit capable of being traversed to in these quick-changing days—to-morrow the boundary will expand. If the memories could expand they would become self-comprehensible and leave us; for, being void to everything below, their expansion would only create *an inner void*, and so evolve to a higher condition. Undue pressure would also evolve this condition into existence.

How to Create an Idea.

By hitting two stones together we create a new idea. A spark is a visible idea. If we could only guide this idea without poles or wires, we could converse with each other without paying a penny. The time will come when this *will* be done, and when it *is* done, the conservation of sunlight will be a universal fact; not, as now, a solitary poet's dream.

Who Originated the Theory?

Nobody ever originated the idea or theory of the persistence of energy. It is silently and almost unconsciously appreciated by all men. The experimentalists have claimed it as a discovery, but though they have demonstrated it to their own satisfaction, they have nevertheless, with all their caution, failed. Rectifying their pernicious error and enlarging their fact-law into a principle-of-principles, I will, in a few paragraphs, expound the mightier law of omnipresent persistence.

Dissipation of Force.

A force can never change its shape or become dissipated. The shape of all forces, unconnected with other forces, is vortical or circular. When force possesses *will* it can act upon its inferior expression, and can therefore change its shape.* But the talk of "dissipation" with or without will is absurd. Take a bubble, for instance, the commonest idea of "dissipated energy." A bubble is first evolved by the presence of motion's void or mind. This rises to the surface a diminutive and whirling globe of air. On arriving at the surface the globe bursts. Is the interior force dissipated? *No.* The *force* of the bursting is the original force that impelled it onwards or upwards; this, on reaching the air, creates an *apparently new* bubble, which continues its flight *unseen* through the *aerial* ocean, and mounts till it reaches the domain of *most* resistance. All the forces of a bubble mount into the air and are finally (apparently) lost in it. The motion of a bubble is a point of force within it. This force-point is a non-decayable solid-void that, immovable in itself, rejects the pressure of surrounding matter, and, always contracting and repulsing to that pressure, produces the phenomena of motion. An atom has all motions, for it contracts and repulses so rapidly that it is compelled to swirl round. This makes its vortical centres a pure void or impenetrable solid, both meaning the same.

The Sublime Law.

Now, if force is persistent, so is the *cause* of force. Cause, force, time, motion, being and thought are but different names for one all-pervading idea—for all is one and one is all. But, though things viewed in themselves (apart and isolated from other ideas or qualities) are self-caused and omnipotent, still this is a world of individualities, and everything checks and triumphantly confines the omnipotent aspirations of ones and individualities. Hence, this is a universe of cause and all things are dependent on each other. Now, then, the *cause* of a force must exist, as well as the persisting force in question, for nothing can exist without a cause. But the *cause* of a force must have *its* cause existing in order to manifest itself in the realm of being—aye, and *its* cause, and *its* cause until the law glares on the vision as *the persistence of the whole past!*

Law of Immortality.

There is a law of personal immortality in existence. It is the strongest law that human mind can conceive of, fierce with the dinning intolerance of power. Death is but a fiction of optics, a cool shade from which we emerge victorious, hardier and more terrible than before.

Indestructibility of the Past.

I have said before that the past cannot be annihilated. Use your brain now, for here there must be "no shuffling." In the first place, nothing can be annihilated. That which is apparently annihilated is only annihilated (changed) into something else. To prate of complete annihilation is to babble ; to mock at what little sense one may possess.

---

*It can change *masses* of voids only.

Now, either the past is not annihilated into something else, or it *is*. If the past is annihilated into the present completely, then the past *is* the present ; we are unborn, and Hector strides on the ramparts of Troy. The past cannot be the present, then, otherwise we must deny our own existence. The denial of existence is the strongest proof in the universe of its opposite's reality. Both present and past exist *through* each other but not *as* each other. Annihilate the fact of yesterday's existence and there can be no to-day. If the yesterday no longer exists in *some* shape, idea or form, where can the to-day lean on ? If you abolish the yester-day *completely*, you deny *with truth*, that the to-day ever had a real beginning, and that the memory of yesterday, once true, is true no more, since yesterday no longer exists, Here is a ridiculous paradox ; a self-refuting lie. To abolish the yesterday is to abolish fact, and to abolish fact is to *annihilate the universe.*

The Potential yet Immoveable Condition of the Past.

But the existence of the yesterday to us, is only a *potential* fact ; the volitional self-moving power belongs to the to-day. It is like a wave, a single wave of time or thought, beating onwards to the tick of eternity, leaving its mist behind at every sweep, till, diminished, feeble and slow, it is arrested by the rocks of death, and, flung weakly backwards, strikes its potential mists on a backward track, until it grows into a rushing wave and heaves again with a mightier roar.

How do We Know that the Individual will Know Itself?

We admit, you will say, the indestructible potential existence of the past. Nay, we are compelled to admit that our whole lives are in existence, occupying their own individual spaces and times ; but how do we know that these individualities, completely defined and separated as they are, will comprehend themselves ? I grant, you will say (for there is not *one* in the world that can tamper with this iron truth) that our lives exist after death, and also allow that individuality* is secured ; but how do we know that this individuality will *know* itself?

Cause of Individual Self-Knowledge After Death.

Now, although *pure* thought is abolished in expressing itself, it does not abolish what we call thought. *Pure* thought, in abolishing itself, evolves thought into being. I may, perhaps, have called *pure* thought, thought, for the sake of brevity in other paragraphs; the reader, however, will discriminate between. Pure thought is inextension;† expressed thought is extension. An expressed thought is a *stare;* it sees its neighbor from one unalterable standpoint, and can see no more. Therefore the

---

* Individuality is proven by the fact that no two minds, objects or forces, can exist in the same space and time.

† Infinite space is inextension, for *as a whole* it has no bounds, no beginning, no end, no middle, no measurement, and, therefore, *no extension.* Pure thought is infinite space and in the act of thinking we are God. I have here mentioned the rapidity of thought—its speed is infinite and has *no motion.* But its infinity is abridged by other thoughts.

whole past is looking, feeling, and apparently moving, comprehending itself alone in billions of living, changing, yet motionless, pictures.

Why we do not Feel as we have Felt in the Past.

The reason why we do not feel the past is that *we are not the past.* We are only *related* to the past. Yonder man with the gray beard is *not* the puking infant of seventy years ago; he is not even the machine from which his childish ideas were flung. He can only imagine his childhood, or, in other words, he is capable of seeing it only with his *mind's eye.* It is impossible for us to live in the same space and time as the past; we cannot do it; *hence we are not the past.* If we could live in the past, we would cease to live in the present, and as we always *do* live in the present, it is pretty positive proof that we do *not* live in the past. We lead a dual existence, for, as I said before, *all things are dual* —the present comprehending a small portion of the illimitable past, the past comprehending itself alone. (LATER, OUR PAST ACTIVITY COMPREHENDS THE PRESENT. THIS IS A GREAT TRUTH.) At death, the past, with a shock, comprehends its complete existence, the commonest mind being a *thousand* times greater than Shakspeare. And now I take my leave of that exalted body, that sublime maelstrom of emotions,

" Whose horrid image doth unfix my hair,
And makes my seated heart knock at my ribs,
Against the use of nature."

The Cause of Joy.

The cause of joy, like every cause, lies in thought. A rapid flow of ideas is joy. To have a rapid flow of ideas, it is necessary to have a rapid flow of emotion. When this flows in the face of death, it becomes enthusiasm. Everything that interferes with this overflow is pain. Embarrassment, stammering, fear, and other things, stop the flow. One may stammer with joy, but it is a stoppage nevertheless. Laughter is a reaction overborne by joy. Those in whom the flow is excessive are what are called geniuses. These are always *more* sensitive than women. Those without this excess of feeling are *false geniuses*, or lucky men.

NOTE—I have on hand a book that deals with the super-human, and if I can find minds thoughtful enough to comprehend it, I shall publish it hereafter. It deals with changeless truths, or truths lying *behind thought.*

SECRET OF THE SUBLIMITIES.

Sons of the grand ! who scorn to voice the cheer
    Of slow-paced Folly in this puling age,
Where feeble Custom deigns the sickly sneer,
    And dribbling fools decry the mounting sage ;
Strong, in the Night, we'll raise the Future's page,
    That from its rise a holier dawn may glow,
High, in our cheers, we'll toss with stormful rage,
    Waving the path where brighter Morn shall flow,
Ere down we sink and sprawl ; forgotten, dead and low.

   *   *   *   *   *   *   *   *

Where'er a void exists the forces reign ;
    Force is a void—the pow'r that hurls the bomb,
Shrieking in death across the riven plain,
    Where the pale city swims in ruin dumb,
And that which drags within its whirling womb
    The half-drowned seaman—and the lightning's show'r,
Whose cloudy flourish strings in trebling hum,
    The heat-roll bubbling where the red seas low'r;
Void is the force unseen—throned in the soul of Pow'r.

E'en to the whisper of the dainty fan
    Beneath sweet Beauty's breast in fluttering sighs,
Each faint report proclaims the truth to Man
    That long has laughed at vauntful sophistries ;
The tiny plant absorbs its faint supplies
    By viewless suction, and the fierce world's mind
Centres in nought—Go seek it with thine eyes,
    Dotards of Science ! frozen dark and blind,
Whose churlish hands doth grope the crown of Truth refined.

Cold is a force, vast in a midnight chill
    Throughout the depths of trem'lous Space around ;
Strong Heat's negation; its absorbing will
    Sits in the heart of molten suns profound;
Contraction's pow'r ! the worlds that long resound,
    Tossing through Space in fierce revolving glee,
E'en by your void their mighty breasts are bound,
    Else to a stretching waste their fires would flee,
And howl in misty rage through swart nihility.

Prometheus * hail!—pressed by the rush behind,
    Thy whirling apple sinks in air below,
Dragged by the countless voids of Earth refined,
    Drawn in the strength of one retreating flow—

---

* Sir Isaac Newton.

And all, save void, whose giddying soul doth blow
    In stormy reels unto the void afar,
Dark Space, whose call the lighter forces know—
    Faint in the sway that wide pervasions mar,
It drowns; the source of storms, ringed from each burning star.

From stark negation see the truth arise;
    Where *from their opposites all things ascend*—
Now by this truth we'll charge amid the skies,
    Where soaring millions with its pow'r shall wend;
For ev'ry law doth on its voice attend
    With trenchant flourish, and afar shall swell
Where juggling gods their trembling walls defend ;
    And warlike Genius, ringing a greedy knell,
Shall toss their crowns in joy and sweep them down to hell.

Hate is a love by stranger wish reproved;
    From deepest Love doth hellish Hate unfold;
Light is the tempest-whirr of Darkness moved,
    Whilst Heat by motion swims from drowsy Cold;
Life from Decay by ceaseless death is rolled,
    Singing its chaunt along the stretch of Time;
The stormy road, from conflagrations old,
    Rained from the clouds, when to a quick'ning rhyme,
The mist of life swept high in raving Hell sublime.

All void is Matter, save by Motion changed;
    Time was a void, merged in the black profound;
Motion is Time, whose force eternal ranged
    Where Chaos yawned and frozen Space was drowned;
A blank Unknown, its boundless waste around
    The change of Time amid the darkness wooed;
Inseparate voids* by fiercest marriage bound;
    Unblent as One; by Imperfection brewed,
The swirling atoms dreamed where drowsy Space renewed.

Time is Decay, and Heat is Time alone,
    The soul of Motion—reddening in its sway
Where Matter, sundered, with a living moan
    Trembles to death, or bursts in molten spray,
Hued in fierce glories, as the face of Day
    Whose torrid frown doth pierce the fainting skies;
All motions first evolved by faint Decay,
    That slept in wastes where far the boundless flies,
    Hailing that shoreless void where morn shall ne'er arise

NOTE.—This poem was dashed off in a short time to give my discoveries (with the rest of the poems) to the public. I have since added my prose, and so insert this because it has a few ideas strongly expressed.

---

* What the reader styles a void is, in reality, two voids joined. A void that is penetrable is elastic, and elasticity ensues when two voids interblending, create, where they cannot blend, atoms in motion. Were there no atoms, no division, it would be solid. This would occur where there was but one void. *Everything* is dual and there are two kinds of spaces, solid and non-solid. To know space is to know all. (See the Mathematic, preceding.)

I've gazed beyond the swart and frozen womb
  Of hollow Night that stared Eternity
In tireless horror; where the stretching gloom
  Slumbered in cold, and swooned in vacancy;
Darkness and void; whose palling mystery
  Weighs on the sense and stupefies the mind—
And such was Matter; yawning drearily
  For countless aons, dim and unconfined,
While Time crawled dreadly on, where Deus* ne'er designed.

DARKNESS DECAYED—and with its fall began
  A silent motion, whirring faint and slow
In viewless rain, until Time's moody span
  Shuddered in trillions; and its myriad throe
Quickened and thrilled in one dark show'ring flow,
  To a far centre where the Darkness clung
Most in sweet love; and in a toss of woe
  Tuned the loud gas, till fierce Creation rung
In wide explosive war where burning chaos sung.

All-wondrous love!† In flourishings and strains,
  Hymns your vast pulsings through the distant blue.
When Progress from Night's brooding cloud regains
  Far-pressing splendor ; If the dullards knew
The swelling pomp that speeds before the view
  Of hardy guagers, they had ceased to sneer
At Nature's laws that blaze the Future through ;
  Whose fearful grandeur spurns this infant sphere—
Proud Foolery shall crouch, for stormful Truth is near.

Ravens of Comte ! Dark nihilistic horde !
  In trampling death your puny facts go down ;
While scornful Truth, where swollen Pride has roared,
  Shall stem your thousands with victorious frown—
Huns of old Error ! soon your gods we'll crown
  In huge derision ; spurning their bodies oe'r ;
Gods of sick France ! your battered powers we'll drown
  'Mid weary ruin—Truth again shall soar !
Then brood its warring cry, " Comte and his school's no more !''

*The writer refers to Jehovah, the Elohim of the Jews. The writer believes in the Great Omnipresent Thought working through Its own unalterable laws—the *designing* laws of Nature.
  †Love is gravitation's force. A human being is only an aggregation of atoms, and he obeys the great sexual law as well as the rest of the creation.

COMPARISON BETWEEN THE ANCIENT MAGICIANS AND OUR MODERN PRESTO'S.
1981.
  After an exhaustive and—might I say it?—*profound* study into the merits of the Egyptian magicians, I am compelled to admit that in the province of *magic*, our American presto's over all bear the bell. Now while the savants of Pharaoh could *apparently* change a rod into a snake or crocodile, *our* presto's by sprinkling some flour-dust over a lump of chalk can make a loaf of bread *in reality.* In fact, so export have our magicians become, that the antiquated and fogyish notion of food has been entirely superseded—while our fathers erroneously imagined that the vegetable and animal kingdom furnished our main staple of reliance, *we* (and we have reason to be proud of it!) on the contrary, have *demonstrated* that the *mineral* kingdom furnishes the proper nutriment of man. Thus, while that idle milksop, Pharaoh, died of swallowing too much sand and water, that same sand in our mouths becomes more

1881.

FRAGMENTS OF "THE O'NIELL."

A DRAMA IN FOUR ACTS. (Rough Draft.)

London—A Street. Enter Civilians.

FIRST CIV.—Good morrow, friend; the town's astir; belike you are for the procession?

SECOND CIV.—Aye, so be I—they say that Shane doth pass the road with crowds of Irishry ; I promise you a rare sight, in faith ; the King of Barbary is nothing to this wild Owneyl.

THIRD CIV.—Godsblood, a very savage! I have heard some honest men declare that he partakes of mangled wolves, and eats of human flesh.

SECOND CIV.—Aye, so he doth; nothing is too fearful for the name he bears. A bloody hand, that shakes of turbulence, glares upon his banners; and yet, egod, he bears himself as stiffly withal as any Lord of Leicester. Though his heart be wolfish, sour and hard, he struts in airs as any Castilian Don—a sort of fury in saffron, who rakes his sword aground, and clatters his shield with blustering hardiness. Well is he nicknamed "Shane the Proud," for he is the most boisterous blade in Christendom.

FIRST CIV.—Egod! he is a rascally churl.

SECOND CIV.—Yea; and as bare-legged as an Highlander, surrounded by a troop of Kernes as fierce as cannibals; by St. Anne, a frowsy lot, tardy in respect, nor hampered much, I'll vow, by the laws o' the Pale.

THIRD CIV.—Well! come, my masters, we'll to the procession. London's afoot and the route 's alive with faces. Such a crowd! An I saw not to-day a sight for the players, may I go begging of bones! Such faces, and of a tongue so droll; belike they were Spaniards, and yet—

SECOND CIV.—A plague o' the Hispany curs! They are thick as flies, and pry our future strength. But what's o'clock? The day moves.

FIRST CIV.—Two, by the glass; come you along?

THIRD CIV.—Aye, we'll by Marybone. [*Enter a messenger.*] Good den t'ye. Moves the procession?

honeyed to the taste than his fabled sugar. *Butterre*, if the efforts of antiquarians inform us truly, was said to have been once drawn from the teats of a cow, but we have good reason to believe that *our* soap-fat, judiciously seasoned by the tobacco-spits of the employés, surpasses the *butterre* of the ancients as much as our verdigris-root surpasses the tal-ho or *tay* of the Chinese. It is astonishing to believe that an island in the Atlantic was once periodically visited by *famines*—when the ground itself lay temptingly before their eyes!—but that was before the times when the human race profited by the lessons of the Dirt-eaters, and man emancipated himself from meat and vegetables. There was a time when the Mineral Theory (since, of course, everywhere demonstrated) was seriously threatened by the clamors of the deluded populace, but happily the ancient merchants and dealers, with great public spirit, bought up the government by wholesale, and hired the health officials to proclaim the superior merits of swill or distillery milk, thereby reducing our ignorant forefathers to crawl upon their hands and feet—the most graceful, as well as the most natural, position of man.

Mess.—By my hilt, I know not what you call it; but the Owneyl is coming. Pray God for your ribs an you 'scape the crushing; such a crowd I ne'er saw since the coronation. In good troth, he is a most valiant looking man; an these be barbarians, there will be a new mode among courtiers. He hath as brave an eye as any true man ever seen, and a scornful; yet so composed unto a mien so full of royalty, that every action doth beseem him well.

Second Civ.—God hap he shall soon be i' the favor of the queen. 'Tis in report that she is partial to an handsome face. An I were crabbed and harsh, and like a Puritan in love with groans, I'd rail my spleen against the godless times—but a curse on the disloyal ronions!—I wish her luck of him. 'Tis very like we may sweat with the Dons; the sooner the better, say I; and if there be valor in these shirted Kernes, we shall know of it. Come you the way, sir?

Mess.—No; I'll to the Strand—farewell.   [Exeunt.

London. A brilliant Chamber in the Palace. Enter Queen Elizabeth, Burleigh, Walsingham, Leicester, Howard and Train.

Eliz.—Has Shane arrived?

Bur.—Aye, an it please your Majesty.

Eliz.—How looked he, sir, and of what complexion?

Bur.—E'en as my lord of Leicester does, your grace; yet fairer, now that I come to think on't.

Leic.—Fairer! I grant him *fairer*. A red and clamorous knave, who frets the air to malediction; hissing his rage against authority; daring all human laws; and shaking his very axe against the name of God's own sovereignty.

Bur.—He bears himself just like a Roman; proud in aspéct of true nobility.

Eliz.—Hardy and proud! You may go, good Burleigh; how different he must seem from gentle Leicester?

Leic.—By my soul, but there is vast difference!

Eliz.—Aye.

Leic.—Aye! Thou art merry in thy mood; preserve thy shafts for shallower friends. Leicester is now the sport of wide comparison, and every one shall turn satirical, whilst thou may lead, and wound his inner soul with careless jibes——

Eliz.—Leicester!

Leic.—And this, when once I thought we felt alike and knew each other's hearts.

Eliz.—Leicester is grown strange and humorous of late; pride's a most catching element when Leicester's rheumatical.

Leic.—This Irish varlet—this tawny savage!

Eliz.—O merry la! jealousy, is it? Come, good Leicester, thou art surely not jealous?

Leic.—Jealous! by St. Paul, no; jealous, faith! Yet I would I were a barbarian, a wild Orson o' the woods, then might I glad the sight of the proud lady I serve. I should then be marketable, arise in favor with each love-sick dame, and become fashionable; (*Aside*) like red hair.

Eliz.—Nay, you are angry; foolish man! an I have not a notion to pull thine ear. But, say, dost thou remember that summer's evening, when thou wert boatman, and I——?

Leic.—Could I but forget it. But now, thy nature's curdled by the envious rout, foes to the name of simple Leicester.

Eliz.—Nay, but thou hast grown over-proud.

Leic.—Proud, my lady?

Eliz.—Nay, then, thou art too humble for the times; I would sauce them more in accordance with our tastes—be prouder.

Leic.—Pride, your grace, is only fit for queens.

Eliz.—Yea, and for lords, too, an' ye give them scope enough.

Leic.—Leicester is grown faded and unfavorable. Burleigh nods, and Walsingham looks cold; their stomachs chuckling at the checks of the very keepers. What if I am scornful, where scullions are vain, swollen with animosity and feverish conceit. I must not walk, but some of the court pass comment on it, each critic of the other's judgment, never confirming once but on some lewd proposal whose base is "pride," and whose summit's " Leicester."

Eliz.—'Tis but by imitation of their inferiors that the great do know their true condition. Greatness is diffidence till the world seems less; then vanity binds it to the general throng. Mediocrity is strict and personal; only the common are unapproachable. He that is frigid and proud hath never felt the heavings of prophetic blood; vanity is the drunkenness of an open heart; but pride is pale and misanthropical. (*Aside.*) Thus do I flutter the feathers of the fretful Leicester.

Leic. (*aside*)—Forgetful dame! she but describes herself; yet, to bandy words with woman is to task the blustering wind. I must burrow through her vanities. (*Aloud*)—I grant that I have been of humor stern, yet in thy service quick and loyal. When thou dost turn, my pleasaunce is forgot, and all the world's misrepresentful.

Eliz.—Ah, Dudley! thou dost know my nature. Tell me the best cure for jealousy.

Leic.—Thy favor, gentle queen.

Eliz.—That shall depend on thy behavior.

Leic.—And thy love ?——.

Eliz.—Ah, Dudley!——.

Leic.—Dost thou love me still? (*Taking her hand.*)

Eliz.—Come, now; thou art trifling; well—yes. (*Distant strains.*) What is that burring sound I hear, which stirs my sense with breathing melody, drumming mine ears with brassy drones, and setting the air in motion ?

Leic.—'Tis the Irish chaunter, a strange instrument, difficult in play, and peculiar to the northern Irish. A most dulcet clarion, untouched by the lips, and played by the arms and fingers alone. Few can play it, and few do know its keys, but their bards I've heard, and in their hands, it strains more tenderly than the harp or violin.

[*Enter the Lord Chamberlain.*]

Lord Cham.—The O'Niell has arrived, your majesty.

(*Drones and Chaunters : " The Coulin."*)

Eliz.—Now, by St. Jude, they are right welcome. Let them be received with honors.

(*Prolonged roll and flourishings. Drums and trumpets.*)

[*Enter Shane O'Niell, Turlough Lynnough O'Niell, Brian Mac Art O'Niell, the O'Hanlon, O'Gnive the Bard, O'Shiel, O'Breslin, O'Hagan, and smaller chiefs of Tyrowen, followed by a vast throng of kernes and gallow-glasses, wearing flowing locks or coulins, dressed in saffron shirts, and carrying battle-axes and swords.*]

SHANE—Dread queen, Tyrowen hails thee! (*Flourish.*) Thy fame resound beyond the limits of dim Neptune's guard, reigning, to light the chivalries of illumined ages. (*Flourish.*)

GALLOWGL.—Hail, all hail!

SHANE—Renownéd be thy laws; puissant be thine arms, reflecting to the farthest future thy resplendent majesty. Live, mighty sovereign, greater than beauteous Maeve; live, the champion of thy friends, the admiration of thine enemies. Rise, just in thine all-inspiring benevolence, guardian of the brave. Be thou monarch of Ireland's heart, till, at the name of England's queen, the hills shall rise from Avonbwee to Dun-na-gall, while drum-rolls muster the multitudinous clans, rousing in fluttering steel, their war-swell waving, shouting the stormy cry, *Friends to Elizabeth, and foemen to the world!* (*Flourish and acclamations*) Rough be our ways, nor tunéd to the music of long-delivered courtesies; tutored in blows, our smiles do frown in scorn; yet our swords can wake as loyal a song when wedging through conflict and stemming the rough infantries, as flattery never woke, or thrummed the symphonies of Italy. We come for justice, and we tender life. Hail, to the mighty Elizabeth, mistress of the nations!

GALLOWGL.—Hail, all hail!

ELIZ.—Brave Chief, we thank thee for this loyal show ; thy words are as warmth unto our hearts. Dear to our blood is the welfare of thy fervid land, the good right arm of England's future glóry ; though long disturbéd by unrestful broil, seek we the furtherance of our large desires in gentle and beneficent rule.

GALLOWGL.—Elizabeth ha-ru ! Elizabeth ha-ru !

ELIZ.—Howbeit, entrust we the advancement of our plans unto the chieftains as yet reluctant ; gladly enow I trust in their adherence.

SHANE.—Adhere, bright queen ! by the haft of Brian, but they shall adhere. Nor long the O'Donnell's flaunt their banners in the glynnes, or the stiff Redshanks mock the hills of Antrim.

ELIZ.—Thou wilt not suffer these rebel Scots to issue forth upon the lands of the Pale ; they grow hardier from lack of policy. But private audience shall enlarge our direction, and I have much to press regarding the Antrim Scots. Thou claimest still the titles of the Irishry ; the proving of our designs shall meet a higher reward.

LEIC. (*aside*)—Now bites the hot itch within the saffron ; let him scratch until his ribs enlarge for title. 'Tis the sore of these Irish. Now, Shane, go crop thy head and turn flatterer.

SHANE.—How ?

ELIZ.—Thy father wast Earl of Tyrone, was he not?

SHANE.—Aye, the perjured !——.

TURL. LYNN (*aside*)—Shane !

ELIZ.—And thou?

SHANE.—The O'Niell ! ! and loyal though I be, regardless of a prouder in this title-loving land. [stir.]

TURL. LYNN.—Oh, Shane ! thou art undoing thyself.

SHANE. (*wildly*)—Not I, in faith ; they did not mean the O'Niell at all.

LEIC.—By what right, dost thou claim the title ?

SHANE. (*angrily*)—By very good right ; (pressing his hilt) by Tanist Law, Sir Saxon—nor bastards stood upon the shields, when I turned, girt by my clan, upon the rath of Tullogh Oge. [*Enter Hugh O'Niell.*] (*Aside.*) Mathew's son here ! I must be wary in the fox's den.

LEIC.—The savage comes out; he bows—ha! but rebellion smoulders in his very eyelids.

ELIZ.—Yet shall he be my friend. (*Smiling at Shane.*) Thou art quick and valorous, and thy nature's to the field, yet for this do I number thee among my captaincy. Belike you prove a friend, our state applauds thee in a just return.

SHANE.—I do desire no more, your greatness. Accept the fealty of Tyrowen's clans. (*Chieftains wave their banners, above which is unfurled the standard of the Red Hand. Shane draws, lowers his sword, and bowing, retreats to his left.*)

ELIZ.—Methinks I have seen that face before. Who is that noble looking boy?

LEIC.—That is the son of Shane's bastard brother Mathew, Baron of Dungannon by succession's right, whom Shane did slay in battle. He is a toward stripling, most honorable of action; an he were not o' the blood of Shane, he were the right man in the shirting of the O'Niell.

ELIZ.—Thy name, fair youth?

HUGH.—Aodh O'Niell—Hugh, and it please your majesty.

ELIZ.—Hugh O'Niell—is he not a goodly boy? An I do not bethink him well, may I be fooled in the sight of Christendom. (*Aside.*) Shane, too, is noble, but of action tempestuous, and may change at the blowing of any wind; but this courtly stranger hath my secret trust; if Shane turns round I shall bait him with this youngster. Curse me, but I half love the sweet varlet already.

HUGH (*aside*)—How flushes that vain face! With what admiring narrowness she scans me o'er. And yet, there is fascination in those sagacious eyes; I see advancement in every glance—she is handsomer than they say of her. (*Aloud.*) Your devoted subject. (*Bends down. Eliz. smilingly allows him to kiss her hand.*)

ELIZ.—Sweet boy, an it be pleasing, thou wilt tarry in England?

HUGH.—Shall I, your majesty?

ELIZ.—Aye, an you like it well.

HUGH.—Like it, beauteous queen!—

ELIZ.—And thou shalt see me yet again, and often; and thou shalt be my friend. Dost thou know what friendship is?

HUGH.—Your majesty!—

ELIZ.—For the present then adieu.

(*Hugh falters and bows off. In passing he meets the stare of Shane. Both finger their hilts. Shane is repressed by Turlough Lynnough. Exit Hugh.*)

Shane, thou shalt come to our audience at twelve. I do hear of new uprisings on the borders. Thou wilt be on hand?

SHANE.—Even so, your majesty; I shall be there by the glass. (*Aside.*) What is now in the wind? Has Hugh been here to tell of news alone? The air grows thick with plots; they darken around us, heavy as night-fall.

> I did outwit the Deputy, and he comes,
> Belated, with a well-blown tale, across
> The tardy seas. Yet I must hasten lest
> His presence fouls, and toss his less'ning name
> For public mirth beyond the ways of Divelin.
> Once in Tyrowen I shall press my sword
> Against the Scotch, renewing of my grudge;
> And if these Saxons push and crowd us then;
> With bloody swords we'll make the Saxons reel,
> Erin shall hope from Niall's conquering steel.

(*March. Drones and chaunters—"Let Erin remember the days of old." Exit Shane and his Irishry.*)

A SCENE ON THE COAST.   (Enter Hugh O'Niell, disguised.)

Now, Neptune, blow your gentlest gales and waft
Them safe across the wandering road.
Adieu to thee, proud hearts; let your sails swell;
Dip to the surges on the petrel's wake;
Wash in the swirls;
You leave but a soldier behind.
Oh, I am harrowed with grief, and faint
Even to the centre of my fixéd heart;
Better that I were in the silent ground
Than mourn the sorrows of this grievous day.
'Tis there my station lies.   There!
Thou bloody hound; thou haggard spawn of hell,
Whose bones are saturate with my father's blood,
Usurping of his son's authority——
Thy sun go down 'mid wrath and cloudy death;
The blight of Conn rave in thy palsied arm;
The slippery sword, knocking a sullen call
On the storm-threshold of thy sundered ribs,
Burrow its ruthless way
To the deepest cavern of thy sunken life,
Thou trebly curst and slaughterous monster;
Yawns the grim tomb for thee, dark Shane-na-dearg;
Whirls the black crown, for thy pale Destiny,
The windy Banshee,
Screams her loud fright upon the Antrim hills——
There's treachery i' the North; thine eyes shall swim
'Neath drowning hafts of blood and war.
                              [*Song re-echoes.*†

Aye sing while ye may.   Ye will cry ere long.
They teach us not to prate of our revenge,
To turn our cheeks and kiss the dastard's hand;
But, by St. Bride, I'd barter Heav'n itself,
And brave perdition, ere I'd stoop and bow
And pledge content even with the all-grinding power
Of hard Omnipotence, drowsing o'er the wrong:
For, lest our fires should sickly feed and die
On barren hopes nodding of other worlds,
And tyrants spawn from sprawling multitudes;
I'd cry thick hatred on the barbarous land,
And stun the dullards with the cry of war.
Accursed be the puling cur that bows,
Striking his coward breast with muttered wrongs;
The worm of proxy, that for mightier hands
Reserves the right to save his fellow man.

---

† A song from a lot of roisterers and sailors that succeed Shane, his forces, Sir John Norris, and others.   The song goes as follows:

> And when 'mid salt our boots will prance,
> We'll show the Spaniards how to dance,
> As round and fine we splash the brine
> And kiss the breeze to land-a.

> Then toast our girls, around we go,
> Nor care which way the wars may blow;
> We are no shakes but jovial rakes,
> Sing hey so merrily grand-a.

Rather than this I'd brave a million deaths,
And bluster in the rugged face of hell;
Face the rough winds, and in the hurried flash
Of dazzling terrors, stare with grislier scorn.
Then what for thee, thou black, night-shaking crow;
Thou gloomy shade, thou horrid swathe of death;
Whose griping claws have torn our draggled house;
And left but one weak voice to pipe its wrongs.
                              [*Song dies on the waves.*

Farewell'; thou false and blood-swoll'n perjurer,
Whose boist'rous veins are drunk with murder;
The raven with his hornéd prow sweeps on,
And with a hardened beak flaunts in his roars,
Obscure and dim, above thy brooding standards.
Fare-thee-well forever ; and with the sun
That sheds his last upon the briny swells,
Drift thou to fearful fortunes;
Whiles drowsy night, in moving rolls amain,
Lights thy lone path with direful omens.
But for thee rough-glibbéd braves and giant Kernes,
Fierce warriors o' the strong and cleaving swords;
Tyrowen greet thee with its loveliest smiles;
Hailing your days with fairer promises,
Bright as the sun whose wondrous rays doth burn
The changeful rocks to ruby-crumbling gems.
Oh, would that I were with them and among
The glad O'Niell's; free as the hawk that dips
O'er the cloud-hills, dizzily and high?
Alas, 'tis but a wish ; an idle prophecy ;
A dream within a dream.
The queen is gameful, and her ways are deep ;
As hard to fathom as the sounding flood
Which flings its rainbows o'er yon slumbering rock,
That travels lingering with sorrowing wails,
To desolate seas and windier worlds.
Upon what strand my fortune casts me,
Alas, I know not ;
No more than the poor wanderer that wings
Him far, 'midst billows, to the flying sun ;
Flapping the sprays on drooping pinion,
His vigor spent, and, fluttering with faint hope,
Too distant to return. Out, out, such thoughts ;
The dread reminders of the poet's life ;
Which, mounting in its joys, trills high' i' the sun—
And drowns beneath a wilderness of waves.
Oh, 'tis a curse to live beyond the times ;
A weary strife, or a contemnéd scorn ;
Better to screen life's taper from the winds,
Than waste its light upon a crowd of slaves.
Yet, by the saints, there's something still beyond ;
A horrid reach ; a vast and glorious end ;
Which burning high, shall dim this tardy age
With fierce and mouldering grandeurs.
Now with my point, I'll touch the voice of Fame ;
But where begin, and what must Niall play ?
If I should linger in the Saxon's realm,
And with base dalliance drowse my lusty prime,
The bards will curse me for a " Queen's O'Niell,"
And cowards vaunt me in the general scorn.

Oh, Shane, thy craft hath served thee out of rule ;
By arts you thrive, by Turlough's aim you die.
There do I see the future's purpose wrought,
Whiles patience broods on opportunity.
Be Turlough fit successor to the proud !
Turlough! poor shadow of my blazing sires !
Well shall I serve my needful 'prentice time
Whiles here I stay, admired o' the fickle queen,
And fostered in fooleries. E'en as the juice
Of sweetest flowers be their compliments,
Were they not drugged and dangerous
As harlot's wine. And this is gentleness,
And noble courtesy; where all's unbarred
Save th' expression of an honest emotion !
By Patrick's wand, I shrink me from the boors,
With all their smell and airs of royalty,
As if their patents came from drunken clowns,
And their sick titles got from yesterday :
For, gazing from these churlish blades afar,
I look towards kings, like gems amidst the rough ;
Feeling the brighter flame that aye surrounds
The deeper meaning of an Irish chief.
There in my sight swells fading honesty,
Mirthful to death and hot as the burning noon ;
Farewell, fierce wanderers, let your songs troul,
Dwelling with gladness on the weary sprays ;
Your hearts are jocund ; and your oars in tune :
But I, forgotten by my father's clan,
Under the winds lament my fortune's ban ;
Forced with a smile to hide my secret moan ;
And sadly wend my hopeless ways alone. [*Exit.*

TYRONE BORDERS. A WILD GLEN.

[*Enter Shane O'Niell, Turlough Lynnough O'Niell, O'Gnive the Bard,
and Irish Forces with Prisoners in their train*].

TURL. LYNN.—Now may the day fall gently on us ; I am spent of humors,
   and I do weary of these bloody incursions.
SHANE.—Aye, and so do I. But all is past, and nought can longer fret our
   hearts with strong resistance.
      Thrice have we pursued the Scotch, and thrice
      Have our swift strokes gone hardy against their power ;
      Now do their scouts lie mould'ring in the glynnes ;
      Their tartans fluttering to the kites and crows ;
      'Midst lonely ways where mournful Death confounds,
      Hoary with ruin and crowded horror.
      Now do their chieftains crawl among the caves ;
      The lonesome kindred of the shagged wolves ;
      Hooting their night-songs to the wintry moon,
      Where Famine screams amidst the rafters.
O'GNIVE (*aside*)—By Christ, I fear this bodes some bloodier ill ;
      These Antrim Scots were all true Irish born.
SHANE.— Thus perish the stout Redshanks, the banshees
      Of a troublous pow'r. There let the braggarts rot,
      And putrefy the land. And now for peace ;
      I am sick o' the hectic pulsing of war:
      Onward my Kernes; strike up your marching tunes ;
      Flourish and advance ; let the *Red Hand* wave,
      Breezy to the whistling wind that sings

Our answering cries into the crowded walls
Of mossy-tow'red Benburb.
[*Enter Messenger and his escort.*]
MESS.—A message, Sir Chief, from *the Castle.*
SHANE (*reads*)—From Divelin—Divelin! by Conn o' the Fights
    I cannot move without this Divelin.
    Sir Henry Sydney—Norris—and English;
    Sheriffs and boroughs, watches and castles.
    And these be the aids you send?   Am I to broil,
    Sweat, and welcome forth your wolves,
    Your brisk adventurers, to hold my land?
    Now by the cross, the emblem of the world,
    The mournful tree where died the best of men,
    Whose dying groan turned black the pitying sun,
    Darkening the globe that senseless Man might live,
    Nor sink to death the witness of such sorrow—
    By that dread Pow'r, the mention of whose name
    Shakes the profound where devils roar and yell,
    I turn for vengeance and the just man's wrong.
    Draw every one, and let your battle shout
    Rend in the air—till Peace flies shrieking hence,
    And Saxons vaunt no longer thro' the land.
SOLD.—   Lammh dearg aboo!   Lammh dearg aboo!
    Lammh dearg aboo!
MESS.—   Pardon, Sir Chief, I but herald the wish
    Of my superiors.   Sir Henry Sydney—
SHANE.—   The rotten gangrene fester in his heart ;
    May he be gripéd in the fangs of hell ;
    The poisonous venom wither up his life,
    And his foul brain send plagues upon his kind—
TURL. LYNN.—Shane—Shane!   Why man, the words fly from thy tongue
    As if thou hadst but Connaill for thine enemy :
    Thy words will be construed into rebellion ;
    The queen, perhaps,——
SHANE.—   Turlough give way, or, by this bloody axe,
    I'll turn thy head to batten in the dirt,
    And send thy body, even where ye stand,
    Under the raven.
    Turn thee hence O'Gnive, nor stir my vengeance
    With thy pale foolish looks, against all minstrels.
    Look to this, and read it ; then if ye blench,
    This warlike clan's in want of fools alone,
    For men with swords must take to other lands.
    Come, messenger, give out thy vantages ;
    Be brief, I tell thee.
MESS.—   Sir Chief, the conditions of the Deputy
    Are writ in the parchment.
SHANE.—   Why, there are no conditions—is this all ?
MESS.—   All, Sir Chief.
SHANE.—   This parchment, sir, was fleeced ere it was used ;
    This ink was drainéd from the strong oak's side ;
    And now, 'twill fleece us to our stunted bones ;
    And eat us up till hunger tears the dead.
    I'll have this parchment soaked in English blood ;
    And write my message with a point of death ;
    Into your homes I'll thrust a deadlier scroll,
    Where the dull raven croaks upon your doors.
    Who is this deputy, that steals his march,
    And in our absence flocks upon our lands—
    Tyrowen—O'Niall's beautiful Tyrowen—

To sheriff the land of Brehon and of Bard,
To crop our heads and *diminish* our store?
Hath not England riches? and doth she need
The cloaks of our half-numb and frozen shepherds?
I tell thee we are poorest that ye know;
Our shrunk stomachs cry at the wit of our hearts;
Then why com'st thou to us with ceremonies?
Niall would be kind,
But Nature starves where bounty alone would flow;
Then, Saxon, what can'st thou demand of us?
Ye, who are richest in all wordly favors!
Could no spot in the big world suit your lust
But Tyrowen? Tyrowen is Niall's land;
The land of Owen the Red; we are lords
In Tyrowen; we, the O'Niells o' the North.

SOLD.— F'yarro an Gall!
SHANE.— And this for Sydney.
Tell him that we are freemen here; scornful
Of Saxons and shakers of battle-axes.
Tell him that his drum's dead roar shall be
Limited and out-braggéd by the swing
Of our war-bells; rocking their long voices
From hills aflame, till the glaring towers
That rise when the red sun is arched o'er hell,
(Sinking his gold in deep abysms of flame)
Grow wan and sickly 'mid the watch-fires hues.
Now do I hear the muttering of the Joyces,
And the call of battle from O'Sullivan's land;
The air is thick, and wrath is brooding nigh,
Heavy with the quake of up-reaching Murder.
Thou occupy my land!
Thou, with blustering threat and railing tyranny,
The parlous couriers of your troubling drums,
To fright our coulins with a brawler's song,
When the wide land is hoarse for bloody swords;
Never shall the sun appear till these clouds
Are cleft and broken, until Sydney falls,
And my clutching hands gripe in 's dabbléd hair;
Never till the Pale is drenched, and Divelin smokes,
Black'ning the red ground.
Our very boys will fright ye with curses;
Our women stun ye with stones; Age himself,
Mumbling of wars, shall babble in the van,
And with his tarnished sword, stemming presumption,
Write his record afresh i' the cannon smoke,
Till ancient fame heralds his familiar stroke
Where forth he strides; lordly, 'mid staggering death.
It shall be war till Mercy herself swoons dead
With horror; aye, till Famine grows childish,
Raving with the slain. It shall be war
Until the earth yields but the fainting sound
Of rotting armor; till the land's become
The sport of ruin, and owls, long hoarse, grow dumb
With shrieking. Our slaughterous arms,
Dripping with sacrificial hate, shall cleave
Until our axes are blunt with butchery;
Till our firm hands, hardened with the pressure
And crush of usage, beat athwart your helms,
And pound on your iron brows.
And com'st thou, Saxon, to fright me with scrolls,

Or hope with pens to battle my warlike Kernes?
Why thou hast got poor solace for thy pains!
And for thy message but a soldier's scorn.
Then come no more if thou art fond of life,
For thou art Saxon, and I hate the Sassenach.
That name, ill-boding and horrible,
Boils in my blood like a vast hell of growls;
Shaking me with a wild delirium:
I see it writ in the skies above me;
Upon my thirsty sword unstained:
Visioned i' the listening blankness of the night—
In the shrill terrors of the vaulting clouds.
SASSENACH! O thou term of skulls and graves;
Thou bitter cry; thou fell suggestion
Of a redder world — the murderer's chain
Swings SASSENACH to the wind.
Go back to Sydney; go back. Tell him
That the Red Hand will dance beyond the Pale,
Shrouded with doom and swirling with carnage.
Tell him that ere the moon's red targe appears,
The clans will pour like thunder to the field,
While their wild ABOO'S, massed in tempestuous cheers
Will knock at the capricious clouds,
And startle their echoes unto England.
Words be your study,
Tricked in the fine diplomacies of the hour:
Niall shall be brief, — take this our answer.
                    [*Hurls down his battle axe.*
SOLD. —   Lammh dearg aboo! Lammh dearg aboo!

A LONG INTERVAL OF TIME. SCENE NEAR DUNDALK.

ENTER SHANE, CHIEFS AND SOLDIERS—RETREATING.

SHANE.—May God's red anger blast them in their halls; may the Black Death nourish them. Would that I had Turlough's head under this arméd heel—ah! Shane, Shane—go, go; go! [*Waves his chieftains back.*]

FIRST CHIEF.—By Saint Patrick's bones, I do suspect this Turlough.

SEC. CHIEF.—Aye, and I. I hate the cur worse than I do the Sassenach.

SHANE.—Aye; go on! go on! O God that all should have stood stiff like stones, and not a chief respond unto our call. Why, the field was scarce worth the crossing of a clan, yet Turlough, like one i' the ague, did turn and wheel before this peevish Sarsfield and his runagates.

THIRD CHIEF.—By Crish la, I suspect the coward for a traitor.

SHANE.—Not one alone, but all were traitors.

SEC. CHIEF.—Nay, it was Turlough—

SHANE.—I say all, all, all!

FIRST CHIEF.—Not all, Sir Shane.

SHANE.—What! Didst thou come forth, or like a lazy bear stood rubbing of thy sides? (To Sec. Chief.) And thou? (To Third Chief.) Where was thy sept? Not one did stir; the very bush would move before their spears.

THIRD CHIEF.—I tell thee, Shane, that I was on the field.

SHANE.—Thou liest—

THIRD CHIEF.—Nay, then, since thou art quick to doubt, thou shalt have thy meaning. I, for one, shall stand this no longer.

FIRST CHIEF.—No, nor I [*going*].

FOURTH CHIEF.—By Jesu, Shane, thou shalt know of us in a change of humor.

SHANE.—What, *thou?* [*Fourth chief dashes his collar down; the rest strike their shields, and exit.*] Now fare ye well, traitors to Shane and enemies to Erin. Friendship adieu, and trustful faith be banished now forever. We are but barks with hailing bells, that meet in the night of two eternities, whose faint "All's well" the darkness cheers, to never sound again.

LONDON. A DRESSING ROOM IN THE PALACE. ELIZABETH
AND HER MAIDS DISCOVERED.

ELIZ. (*trying on a wig*)—By my troth, it is an arrant piece of roguery;
and yet it becometh the head as rich as its price. An I do not
mend mine attraction in the sight of followers, their 'haviour sinks
be I never so royal. Heigho! for the times when I was coy and
blithesome; my face is wrinkled, and I am fretted with ceremonies.
(To the first maid)—How long is it since thou didst see me blush?

FIRST MAID.—I—I don't remember; I—my mother—!

SEC. MAID.—What shouldst thou remember, silly girl? Ah! your grace,
thou didst not maintain thy color when last thou sawest young
Essex; indeed thou didst redden even as a young country girl.
What should such a wench as thee know of blushing? When thou
art a woman of quick virginity, and as unconscious of thy charms
as thy mistress, thou shalt know the confusion inherent to maiden
blood. Pardon, your grace; thou wert born to exalt our frailer
kind—shall I darken thine eyebrow a little? Ah! that was a gentle
stroke, and a graceful; marry, thou art fitter than all i' the realm
to reign Queen Beauty over an handsome and a merry land.

ELIZ. (*delighted*)—Think'st thou so? Ah! woman, woman; thou canst
talk as man; but tell me, dost thou bethink me as fair as the de-
posed Queen o' Scots?

SEC. MAID.—Well, I vow, there be points of resemblance atween ye
that maketh comparison keen and discriminate, and yet, were I
arbiter between the handsomest of my days, my voice should voice
its parting breath for England and her Queen.

ELIZ.—Oh, you pretty flatterer! And now Mistress Silence, why art
thou mouthing thy solitude unto the wall? Come hither; why
thou art growing as loose i' the face as this Juliet i' the tale—what
is the matter with thee?

THIRD MAID.—An it be pleasing to your grace, he, he! the girl is in
love—hee, hee, hee!

SEC. MAID.—Aye, and they say with a most pretty gentleman. [*Goes
off laughing.*]

ELIZ.—In love! Art thou in love?

FIRST MAID—I do not know.

ELIZ.—Do not know? marry, thou dost not know. Dost not? Godslife, thou wilt know, perdy!

FIRST MAID [*Imploringly*]—Your majesty!

ELIZ.—Away, thou deceitful jade. In love, certes! By my troth, thou
art in love with half the gallants in the town. [*Third maid turns
her face.*] Some tavern Knight, I'll warrant; thy father shall

know of it. An ye tell me—come prithee, is it none within the Palace? Perhaps I do know him better than thy fancying.

FIRST MAID.—I do love none of the town ; nor e'en of England ; nor do I love any of foreign appearance ; none, none.

ELIZ.—Thou art a stubborn wench, but I shall sound thy preference. Thou art an hypocrite, a flattery-lover, a kisser of men ; [*maid weeps*] get thee away ! thou repentless girl, away ! For what must we believe nowadays. Nothing but loving ; as if the world had nought to do but swing to the glueing of lips ; while wisdom, flouted, stands gazing and giddy, the scoff and merriment of every jigging fool. Wert thou ever so situate as to feel thy reason fluttering on the breast of some of these noble Fitz-Champions ?

SEC. MAID.—I, your grace ! No, thank my good fates ; I do not see how any sensible maid could love these whiskered gallants ; 'tis nought but a weakness unnatural.

ELIZ.—And thou, coulds't thou so lose thy maiden regard as to plight thy troth to a man—well ?

THIRD MAID.—He, he ! your majesty, not for the world ; he, he !

ELIZ.—I thought not. I shall preserve thee from them, then ; and when thou art old thou shalt thank me for it.

THIRD MAID. [*bursting into tears.*]—Y-yes your m-majesty !

ELIZ.—Ha, ha, this is not echo, then. Foolish girl—come, let's be merry again. A knock.

[*Enter Bacon ; standing by the door.*]

How now, Bacon, what is't ye want ?

BACON.—Great empress————

ELIZ. [*aside.*]—Empress ! he begins well.

BACON.—I do beseech thee to look upon this scroll, hoping thou wilt pardon the hour, and extending gracious interest in thy suitor's behalf————

ELIZ.—What, another preferment ? Twice have I told thee, no ; now e'en to the third time do I answer, no. Begone ! when I bethink me of preferment I shall tell thee so. [*Exit Bacon.*] Marked you the studied servility of this man, this Latin prater, this master of learning and saged foolery ? With what complacency he lays his points, squaring his ground for checkered argument ; with what cold proverbs he bestrews his secretive way, raising his finger as a dissentient parson droning o' the Bible ; withal so deep that he forgets the turning of his nine issues ; yet smiling, hints of indefensible oppositions ; the lesser the knowledge the greater the smile, till the tired sense following in a maze of the commonplace, comes back to start, or dulls in a whirl of mock profundities. And this is Master Bacon—nothing but self, preferment, and offices. Godslife ! I am sick o' these offices ; nor time, place, or the privacy of our state, protect us from them. But I would return to nature ; tell me what you all think of Tyrone ?

FIRST MAID—Hugh O'Niell ?

Eliz.—Ah! Yes, Hugh, the nephew of that rascally rebel Shane, who was murdered by the Antrim Scots. What dost *thou* think of him?

First Maid (*startled*)—I have never seen him, your grace.

Sec. Maid—Oh, I think him as pleasant as any ever seen; such a beautiful set of teeth—

Third Maid—And such a pretty mouth.

Eliz.—Beautiful teeth, and a pretty mouth—is that all?

Sec. Maid—Oh, I think he has the prettiest foot in the world.

Eliz.—And this their conception of a man! A pretty tooth, a mouth, and a foot! Why, as sure as there groweth little apples, thou art both as silly as sheep o' the Downs. A cat may have all these; thou beginnest like a cat a-chasing of his end. Where are his eyes, his nose? Call you this judging of the beautiful? Where the lines of his valiant brow, th' unselfish curve? Go to! thou art of the shallower sort, full o' the fashion. [*Third maid whispers.*] Who? Tyrone? Admit him. Begone!

[*Exit Maids; First Maid lingers, and slowly departs.*]

ON ROSSI'S FAILURE.

1882.

Sing all hail to noble Rossi! long the futures will resound
    With a thousand harps rejoicing to the praises of the bard—
I behold thee full of splendor, and thy brows with glory crowned,
    Great and rich in the good God's reward.

But I saw thee in the glimmer, when the house was faint and cold,
    When the fashion sought its level in the sickly halls of crime,†
Where the lisp of cheering Folly thro' the humming dome was rolled,
    And cursed o'er the melodies of Time.

And I saw thee, oh, my sorrow! in a dark and gloomy land,
    Sore with ruin, and neglected, as with gentle face you bowed;
Nor forgetful of the silent few, you soared amidst the grand,‡
    Till our hearts, high with grief, wept aloud.

Then all hail majestic Rossi! for to spurn the coward's wrong
    Does my soul go swooning backwards thro' the misty stretch of years,
And fast-humming from its darkness, swells the loud, expanding song
    Of my life, with its million of cheers.

†A theatre used for the amusement of the rabble, corrupts, by omission of the nobler sentiments, the character of the people. That which is not noble is base. Society produces pitiable, not laughable, characters. To laugh at "dudes" is to bring the insane to jibber for your amusement.
‡The play was "Lear."

AN ARAB'S REPLY.

WRITTEN AT NINETEEN.

My dream is on the billows; and I ride
    Where sprays are glowing through the seas of old;
Bursting through molten clouds, while dim waves glide
    To burning distance where the sun-gates fold;
Dashing resplendent in a waste of gold,
    Swimming through hazy fires far-fading grand,
Rifting the swirl, where colors deep and cold
    Dance into rainbows by the breezes fanned;
    And stranger seas arise beyond the Saxon land.

Such was my first of ocean; and in tears
    I dreamt of England, lost amid the spray;
Sighing my grief, while shook with boyish fears,
    I watched the shrill waves call amidst their play—
My childish dreams are vanished; and I stray,
    With wallet slung, a bard of olden time;
The last to wander on the lonesome way;
    Bending a pinion for a world sublime,
    I turned—but ye could spare the ragged sons of rhyme.

The world has starved, and wrung my heart with pain;
    I love it; e'en though drenched unto the skin
I've sung my hoarseness through the beating rain,
    While drunken Revelry could laugh within.
To lodge where Fever dwells with homeless grin,
    While midnight tempest o'er the gutters drowned,
As hunted, sad and cheerless I stole in
    From drawing pictures on the frozen ground—
    Clutched, ere the wrong I knew, by hemming laws around.

When Treason, urged by swordless Chivalry,
    Swept on the North with honest hearts of gray,
And brothers, crossed in grimful enmity,
    Drenched the red fields where drownéd armies lay;
Exhaustless carnage pouring to the fray;
    Huge commerce rolled amid the gen'ral grave;
And with its fall, wailed famine and dismay
    To the starved toiler far beyond the wave,
    Who cheered for "Stripes and Stars," where dastards
        banned the slave.

Then, on the streets, the poor and bashful child
    Sang his low tune; yet, fierce in mastery,
Uprose 'gainst felon sneers; and strangely wild,
    Stared as Macbeth in drunken tragedy—

"Bind up me wounds!" and e'er in sympathy
  With boundless minds by jealous gods abhorred,
Dread Shakspeare fed their wide precocity;
  Ah! for the few, ranged in a large accord,
  Who wrung from public flags* a scant and cold reward.

Lowest of these, in cruder sweep I soared,
  Scorning all rule, my whirling fingers drew
The Kremlin's rise, where dying Moscow roared,
  Crashing through clouds that burned in glaring hue;
And the pale Corsican, o'er Waterloo,
  Bending his last upon the Armeé's doom—
These were the days when oft I could renew
  A nestling trust in things of earthly bloom,
  And dreamed—while Freedom wept o'er Lincoln's
    bloody tomb.

At five I roved; the War's great tragedy†
  I stole from discourse and a score of songs;‡
Quick was my sense to Europe's history;
  Britannia's heroes and Ierrnie's wrongs ;
High 'mong the gods I stared, where dread prolongs
  The hoarse tragedian, pale in a ranting joy;
Thrilled to my bones, I cheered among the throngs ;
  Renewed his clamor when the nights rolled by,
  And roared on the crowded "'Change"free from the law's annoy.

Against the law my comic art was spread,
  Fighting for life beneath its felon frown ;
Move on! and hounded, in a frozen dread,
  The ceaseless truncheon stared me through the town ;
Beaten and worn, wan hunger bent me down ;
  Drawing my pictures as I crouched in fears,
Till, where the boor in pompous wig and gown
  Nods by old rule, defenseless and in tears,
  I stood, without a crime—condemned, at seven years.

No friends were there when shook the misty hour
  That boomed its echoes upon Cheapside jail,
As, through the crowd, that solemn face did low'r,
  And froze my heart's blood in a hopeless wail—

---

* The flag-stones—the stone sidewalk on which we drew.

† I used to draw the portraits of Washington, Paul Jones, and others before the "Washington Hotel." There were crowds of "Yankees" there, and as they encouraged me most, the pictures of the "Merrimac and Monitor," "Assassination of Lincoln," "Alabama and Kearsage," "Bunker Hill," and the "Great Fight between Heenan and Sayers" were frequenily drawn. At five, I drew crowds of generals, heroes, pirates, murderers, kings, knights, pugilists, lion-tamers, animals, land-scapes, and caricatures. As I could not read, I had to shout their titles. I was surrounded by minds whose originality was limitless ; aye, even *beyond* Shakspeare's. I lament their loss every day of my life.

‡ At five the writer knew over sixteen hundred tunes. I remember all or nearly all the tunes of my father. I played no instrument. I composed as well as remembered, and by instantaneous variation changed and intensified to deeper sorrow the lamonts of my father.

Hemmed by an iron door, wounded and pale,*
  Two days on bread and water there I lay,
Till paid Injustice waved me from the rail; †
  Six years in dread St. George's walls to stay,—
  Whose name shall fright my soul e'en till my dying day.

My back is scored, my strength is broken down ;
  Yet others died, the gentlest e'er I knew ;
Unspoiled by love and reared in fortune's frown,
  Kind, and as Mercy fading, sweeter grew;
Consumption beckoned, and they bade adieu,
  Smiling with lustred eyne unto the grave ;
And low mounds rise where ceaseless yawnings brew
  The vengeful death, where foul contagions rave,
  Whose cloud shall fright the land and blast the pampered knave.

The name of God is useful with the strong,
  And each may quote the Scripture as he feels;
Flaunting the sense that hallows e'en the wrong,
  Where Vice may prove its claim in Virtue's heels ;
Now to Thy name the fainting scholar reels,
  With trampled groan, where pray'rs avail no more ;
While trails the lash where past the Brother steals
  To drown the sickly boy, whose sunken roar
  Shrieks from the wintry flood and rolls to Heav'n's high door.

Ere dwelt my fancies 'neath the Moslem sun,
  Where puny Cáprice doth the mind enthrall,
Whose drowsy life in sleepy pleasures run,
  And nods, unminful of the future's call.
I felt an English bastinado's fall ;
  Till humming blows stunned in the legs along ;
Punished for talking! Let him gasp and crawl!
  While silent fear crept thro' the blanching throng,
  Awed by the Christian arm that swung the leathern thong.

In earlier days, when I was wild and free,
  And rambled void of stocking, hat or shoe,
Shirtless, I laughed in scornful misery,
  Declaiming where the fiercest winter blew;
My feet were hacked with frost, nor frost I knew,
  When shuffling "Richard," with a meaning strange;
With tears unusual o'er a pot of stew,
  If fortune followed in my listless range;
  Cold was the wintry past, yet colder still the change.

*I was so injured in the arrest, that I had to be put into a carriage to convey me to "St. George's." I was struck on the ankle by a truncheon. Ignorance and cruelty go hand in hand, and the finest specimens of completed ruffianism that ever picked a drunkard's pocket, assaulted women, or hastened the exit of a fainting man, are to be found in the Orange constabulary force of Liverpool,
  †The person who convicted me had an interest in my conviction, for he was paid half a crown for the arrest of every homeless boy, by the authorities.

With bloodshot gaze we stared upon the snow,
　　And cried, with feet enlarging, 'mid the frost;
Foul humors spread, and laid the weakest low;
　　While from the cold, their finger joints were lost;
And on our barren beds the snow-whirl tossed,
　　Till Ventilation screamed above the dead;
By rule we lived, nor could those rules be crossed,
　　Till manhood's grief arose from secret dread—
We wept until the child in cold oblivion fled.

Banished from all; faint can the bright world know
　　The trembling griefs burst from a heart's strong love;
Bound to my sunken soul, in ceaseless woe
　　I groaned and shivered to the walls above;
While in my dreams, by future's darkness wove,
　　I saw my brothers blowing wide and far,
Ploughing the years, in distant seas to rove;
　　And him, the brightest, through the tempest's war,
Fading in ocean waves, drowned, on a floating spar.

My father* perished through the ruffian hand
　　That, by the laws, for senseless tribute came;
Charging support for one 'mid felons banned
　　By needless trial and insulting shame;†
Ruined and gray; hot with the fever's flame,
　　He cursed the bailiff and his crop-eared guards,
Till, in a jail, wan Death renewed his claim—
　　Spurning the clime which freedom still retards,
Then rose great Turlough's son—"the last of Erin's bards."‡

---

* My father was, previous to the birth of his children, the last descendant of Turlough Carling, the most famous of the Irish bards. My grandfather, born in London, was the first to prove his tuneful pedigree; for, in '96, in the streets of Bantry, he struck the first strains of the "Rising," in that rousing and far-famed song, the chorusing, drinking, table-pounding, "starn" and sturdy old "Shan Van Vogh." My father was the author of the "Pauper's Drive," "Village Born Beauty," "Ragged Coat," and other famous songs and poems. He was a strolling minstrel, even when a boy, and could find a market for any of his juvenile productions. He composed over nine hundred songs, often selling them to other parties. In Ireland he composed a great many that were suppressed by the English Government—only one or two garbled versions of his fiery originals remain; such as "By Memory Inspired," etc., etc. My father's best songs, his swelling marches and warring appeals, are unknown—he is one of the lost poets, far superior to any of his predecessors in Ireland, as a bard. In the mirthful my father yet exists, and his humor is explosive enough to set the weather-cocks fainting. It is enough to say that the following were hatched forth from the brain under whose fostering care the "Wonderful Duck" quacked, and the "Turkey Cock" first learned to crow: "Nell Flaugherty's Drake," "Wedding of Ballyporeen." "Paddy Haggerty's Owld Leather Breeches," "Irish Schoolmaster," "Irish Teacher," "Doran's Ass," "Digging for Goold," "Oh, the Great Big Irishman," "Botherin' Rakes of Derry," "Ducky Little Stirabout Pot," "Donneybrook Fair," "Cruiskeen Lawn," "Arrah, give me the River Shannon or I'll Die with the Drooth," "Oul' Bog Hole," "Biddy of Sligo," "Rattling Boys of Paddy's Land," "Larry O'Brian," "Paudheen Rhu," "Ochone! Paudheen O'Rafferty," "County of Wicklow," "Judy Joyce the Joker," and scores of others.

† The writer was convicted on the charge of drawing pictures on the flag-stones. Not content with this (seclusion in a walled prison), they tried to make the friends of the children pay to support them. As most of them were cripples and paupers, they had to deny their children or go to jail. My father was taken from a sick bed to jail.

‡ It is a mistake to suppose that Turlough Caroling (Goldsmith's "Carolan the Blind") was in reality the last of the Irish bards. His descendants, nearly all of whom were destined to be born on English soil, not only plied their roving profession, but composed more songs and tunes, that *still survive*, than all the rest of the song-making world (in English) together. To read my father's songs is, of *his* time, the best history extant.

Child of the past! the mountain wild his home;
    He wandered, as his fathers did of yore;
Last of the Brehon race in Eire to roam,
    He waked his harp along the Shannon shore;
And Desmond heard his loud illálu soar;
    From silent raths he made the dastard yell;
Suppression came; but mounting as before,
    His songs across the Western Main shall swell;
Where Brunswick, foul and dark, will hear the future's knell.

Fell,—as the bards, where treason reared amain,
    And freedom's star in bloody wrath was drowned;
Thrumming their harps upon the dark'ning plain,
    E'en where the mournful standards closed around;
F'yarro an Gall! and o'er the fatal mound
    Swept their wild death-song to the fading sky;
In blust'ring burrs arose the gleeful sound—
    Where carnage sickened 'mid the whelming cry,
Fiercely their war-pipes screamed, in swirls of buzzing joy.

Sons of the satin robe! in days of old
    Your harps swung high in Tara's ringing halls;
Hearty in love, from drinking horns of gold,
    Tossed the grand pledge round wide Kinkora's walls—
And all, save one, have sunk in quenchless brawls;
    While Error smirks in the dissembling brood—
On foreign rags thy royal vesture falls;
    Last and the least! by stormy Nature woo'd,
I'll raise thy warring strains, fierce minstrels of the rude!

Oft have I dreamed, by intuition led
    Beyond my reason, of the ways of Man;
Craving for brighter spheres, where self was dead
    And wise benevolence eternal ran;
But soul within these bigots ne'er began;
    And Science drivels in this paltry sphere,
Mending the wind around each pigmy plan,
    Prating of Comte, with narrow brow severe;
Fools! if the truth were known, your gods had cause to fear.

Not till thy rule is dead, O man of dust!
    Not till the Law shall rule in Use amain,
Morals evolving from thy selfish lust,
    Shall wide Fraternity, sweet-humming, reign;
Shines a new light upon the toiling train;
    The universal destiny we feel,
When Fashion turns, a heav'n below to gain,
    Allied with Mind, to groove the list'ning zeal;
When ev'ry man's a link to bind the gen'ral weal.

All this forgot—when tied upon a post,
    Head down, while beat with pokers, one was hung;
Drowning his cries, as to the Holy Ghost
    A burst of praise with cursing hearts we sung;
And one since dead, when shadow'd Murder stung,
    Was wrapped, "to save his life!" in flesh of swine
That died from humors, sloughing in the dung;
    And some were washed, all bleeding, in the brine
Left from its swollen corse—the tardy truth be mine!

This flesh we ate; the bastinado calms
    The fainting throbs that fretful hunger knew;
Well could the horse-lash stem the rising qualms
    That turned, o'er daily mess half rotten through;
While scurvy menaced in that fetid hue,
    And starved neglect glazed in each flickering wan;
None would remember! Ah! the silent few,
    Who heard poor Mullins' shriek ere he had gone;
Forgot his mother's pray'r, to point at Brother John!

The years went on; our friends were seldom seen;
    None came for me; the last was cursed away;
Too ragged; his sad presence would demean
    The forcéd primness of our starved array,
In friendless fears we waited through the day
    Wearing like torture, as the numbers fall—
And some were rosy; but the lone ones, they
    Groaned in hoarse sorrow at the final call,
And shook with broken sobs against their prison wall.

Far on the desert hums the noonday wind,
    Tossing the panting cries of hot despair;
White with the bleaching skulls of lone mankind
    That rave, deserted, 'mid the burning glare.
Nor books could spin my heated fancies there,
    My weakness felt it when the sun shone high,
And the dead walls flung back the heated stare
    That beat our dizzy brains in fierce July;
  Denied—we drank of ink and drained our bottles dry.

Save on the gentle could those rigors wear,
    Shrouding their mem'ries deep in future woe;
So with the world; its ruthless hand must bear
    On trustful minds all guiltless here below.
Survive ye fittest! till ye overthrow
    The godly brutes that 'gainst the helpless wage.
How dwelt I for one stiff, rebounding blow!
    Nor dwelt I long, for down we hurled the gage,
And roared each rebel voice in stark, tempestuous rage.

Quick to the cry, we trampled on our foes,
    And mad with joy, tossed them in high dismay;
Tore through the clubs, and grimful, as we rose,
    Wresting their staves, we thrashed them in our play;
Now turn ye back and draw the coward's pay!
    Tell how your buttons blazed when rolling near;
Your warlike helmets battered in the fray!
    Till scornful Humor, bounding in a cheer,
Fluttered your valiant hearts, amidst a howling jeer!

A smothered mind points but a future wild;
    They sped, to force in time, the Dardanelles;
At Isandula, red with bodies piled,
    Swept their lone bay'nets to the Zulu yells;
Thought of the Past, when muffled sentinels
    They frowned upon the deserts we had won;
Scornful in death, their bloody "F'yarro" swells;
    Swimming, they stare, as o'er the Afghan's gun
Rattles the cry that rose by Benburb's setting sun.

And such their fate. Poor Airinn still ye be
    The warlike stay of cold Britannia's fame;
While Genius, staunched in distant Tyranny,
    Falls from the true, to boast the stranger's name;
Kindest of owld! be ragged coats your shame!
    Gaze on the crowds where windy havoc dooms;
Varied in hues, the face is yet the same;
    Mounding the trench where cloudy Murder booms;
Grimly their bay'nets whirl o'er stormy Highland plumes.*

Proud,—as an iceberg of the windy North,
    Britannia rose and plunged upon the wave;
Stemming the flood in icy battle forth,
    Whose thunders roared, but large addition gave;
But now, the torrid sky she dares to brave,
    Deaf to the shout that rolls around the world;
Far-stretching glory leads unto her grave;
    "Justice and Right" for Airinn be unfurled,
Or swim the misty death by dark Rebellion hurled.

Speed not the day, when drained by foreign ills,
    A voice may shake her—England yet shall blaze
High in the future war of *human wills,*
    While Irish harps shall thrum with nobler praise.

---

*The writer is above the pettiness of insulting the brave. He means not only the Irish who wear "the bonnet blue," but the grand Highlanders themselves, the Scoti of Erin, who swept the Romans backwards, and drubbed the backs of "the masters of the world." The writer is a citizen of the world, and is provincial only where oppression reigns. True patriotism is love of *man;* all else is local and ephemeral.

Airinn still leads in these barbarian days,
    Stern, in the force of a united land;
Well may the minstrel tune in future lays,
    Of burning names, where peaceful martyrs stand,
    Crowned in a brighter glow than Malachy the Grand.

All Nature's one in lasting union formed;
    Nor tall Presumption can its teachings mar;
Cannons may roll, and Havoc be out-stormed
    In marching thunders of tumultuous war:
Rattle your drums! Your banners flaunt afar!
    From the hot trench let thoughtless Murder wage!
Earth's placid curse survives the vauntful scar;
    Gainers of naught, but heroes of an age!
    To fertilize the land, and feed the future sage!*

Our stout rebellion raged behind my flight,
    While on that wall I laughed unto the sky,
Shaking my fist upon the stretch of night
    As the wan morn rolled mistily on high;
"Richard's himself agen!" and, to the cry,
    I clutched unto the course that stretched below;
Pursued by winds with laughter in each sigh;
    While drummed my coward nerves, till, weak and slow,
    I sauntered where no friend could greet me here below.

Beside the door I sat me down and cried,
    Where strangers laughed; a homeless place to me;
Where last my mother, smiling, ere she died,
    Watched me depart in distant revery;
Houseless I stood, not knowing where to flee,
    And sank, all trembling, with an idle moan;
Then to my soul came freedom wearily;
    Gone were the friends, their mem'ries left alone;
    And broke my future's grief upon that old door stone.

Nought but the skies, whose tears remained unchanged,
    Did pat my front in welcome cold and chill;
The streets seemed small, and blacker, as I ranged
    Past olden haunts and rheumy courts of ill;
The morning cries no more my veins could thrill,
    Their jocund laughter died amidst the Past—
Out in the busy squares they knew me still;
    Menaced by vengeful eyes my lot was cast—
    I drew and braved by night—but I was ta'en at last.

---

*A friend has pointed out that this stanza has been in substance and idea, though not in form, expressed by Byron. If so, it is merely a sympathetic coincidence. To create with me is as easy as to copy, and I do not believe in robbing that which I possess. I would rather imitate him than malign him—let Swinburne know that to criticise *Byron* one must be a *poet!* The individual must sometimes be struck lest a fool should steer the masses.

Two months of freedom! oh, the change it brought!
The rule of Hate among the shadows fell;
By nobler masters were the school-boys taught,*
And softness wrought where brutes had failed to quell;
And kindness rose amid the warring hell,
Leading the stubborn heart by gentle wiles,
Till Emulation waved; and where they tell
Our mental record in reporting files,
High 'mong " The Schools" we rose—first in the British Isles.

Since then I've roamed; my feet have borne me on
Thousands of miles; banned in the vulgar pride
Of the vaunt world that fretful, weak, and wan,
Spurns the lone help by fading Truth supplied.
Eccentric bards! by coward hearts decried,
Honest and strange! frighting their witless fear
To giggling sense from what your sense implied;
Well can you brave the faint and sickly leer,
Till voiceless millions wake and swell your prouder sneer.

With slip-shod heel I've passed the drowsy town,
Where night curs bayed my 'wakening minstrelsy;
Lord of a stone, I've proudly sate me down
And lost my soul in wide astronomy;
Celestial orbs! whose breathing harmony
Rings through the brilliant realms of boundless cause,
Faint in the rune of immortality,
Your voices thrill me in their vast applause,
And stir a fiercer love for Nature's beauteous laws.

A grander sphere exists—nor yet for me;
My blood is youthful, tossing in its fire,
Yet shall it mount on smooth Philosophy,
Winging its dainty flight o'er wild Desire;
Dead to the Past, I hear the distance quire,
Living beyond in boundless love secure;
Thrilled by the sights where man shall yet aspire,
I well can mock the vauntings of the boor;
Years, by the fool abhorred, in heav'nly joys allure.

*Chief amongst the masters was the handsome, soldierly, exalted, poetical and princely Nolan—a born chieftain of men, the rewarder of scholars, fit for a throne upon Tara; a blameless and benevolent bard. The dead are showering blessings on the patron of orphans ; Heaven has a throne for him, radiant with his mercies ; the bards are thrumming his praises.
" May the white sun and moon rain glories on your head,
All hero as you are and holy man of God—."

I notice that in the dearth of poetry a nation turns back to review its songs—a half loaf being better than none. I notice that one Foster has been credited with " Hard times come again no more," and " Don't you remember sweet Alice, Ben Bolt?" For the relief of such dark beggars as Foster and others from the authorship of these songs (making fortunes out of the product of that sublime genius who lies rotting and nameless in a pauper's grave), I advance the truth, and brand these pirates as cowards and liars. Not only did my father write the above songs, but he wrote a bawdy song, called "Jem Blunt," which was in tune and style the forerunner of " Ben Bolt," and as for "Hard times come again no more," it is only the same tune as his "Nelly Gray" in disguise. He wrote several effusions in the latter vein, such as "In the days when I was hard up," and " This grand conversation was under the rose," (all the " Conversations" are his). " Hard Times," the lament of an Irish peasant, was written in Kelly's ale-house, Addison street, Liverpool, in 1849.

54

FAREWELL TO ENGLAND.

WRITTEN AT FIFTEEN.

I watched the pale sky as it welcomed the star
    Of the evening that rose with a glow on our lee,
And gazed on the sea-gulls that flitted afar
    In the light of the sun as it sank in the sea;
And my bark was upheaving, while kissing the spray
    That dashed in sweet music wherever it fell,
As, mournful, I bade my adieu to the day,
    And sighed to old England a saddened farewell.

Farewell! and I wistfully dwelt on the wave
    That was wafting me far to the land of the new;
And I felt the sad lot that my poverty gave,
    As the shores in the distance were fading from view;
For the hearts that could bless by the strangers are banned,
    And its fate, o'er the billow, sad prophets will tell,
When England shall mourn for the last of the grand,
    And Genius has waved to a saddened farewell.

The lights in the gloaming burn faintly and dim;
    Our gallant ship's mounting and wooing the wind,
And dashing through billows that dizzily swim
    To the edge of the moon that is rising behind;
While our bow flashes red in the waters below,
    And around us the winds in lone melodies dwell,
Which die on the flood in a sobbing of woe;
    And send o'er the breakers a saddened farewell.

The darkness is on us, and loud the wind roars;
    The noise of the water is heard all around;
The moonlight has vanished, the sweet whited shores .
    Have swam thro' the dashings that solemnly sound;
And the cold heav'ns blaze with the stars' throbbing light,
    While my tremulous voice o'er the ocean does swell;
And my beating heart speeds thro' the gale and the night,
    And echoes to England—Farewell, oh, farewell!

NOTE.—*By the strangers are banned.*—Neither the royal family nor the nobility of England are one with the people, for to be *of* the people is considered a disgrace. Therefore these so-called nobles are more foreign than the foreigners, for the foreigner, as such, will mingle with his fellows as *man.*

PLAINT OF ROSALINE.

1881.

Love hath a nest in my bosom so tender;
    Soft was his eyne as the glance of the fawn;
Unto his wish could my happy soul render;
    Alas! I must weep, for my lover is gone !

Yet I will wander the grassy mead over;
    Sadly I'll sing for my Coolin so fair;
Wanton, why stray from the plaint of your lover !
    Rosaline's heart with my gentle would share.

Bright was the morn when I stood by the bushes;
    Merry the days when we rambled so free;
Strangely entranced, while I thrilled in my blushes,
    Joy to my veins was his welcome to me.

Yet I shall meet him when shines the to-morrow,
    Hailing the lark singing sweetly and gay;
He'll come through the flow'rs and banish my sorrow;
    For he has my heart and can never betray.

He is my love, and my soul he will marry;
    Rosy I'll greet him, nor voice to my pain;
Shadows of night, you but linger and tarry !
    Haste to be gone! I would see him again.

Strangers may come, ah! but nothing can woo me—
    Life's but an hour to the soul that is true—
Time from my loving can never undo me;
    Faster than time shall my loving renew.

THE GREEN BOWERS.

1878.

Hear the cuckoo on the tree,
        In the green sunny bowers ;
And the linnet merrilee
        Whistles, "Come to the bowers."

Will you come to the bowers, where the golden beams are falling
As they show'r among the rich perfume ?
Where the green wings burn, and each dulcet voice is calling,
Trilling, *Sweet oh ! sweet*, in flutters 'mong the bloom ;
Where the dying summer wind blows along,
And the merry posies nod to the song ;
Where, in sweetness, their hues in a million tints are glowing,
Welling beauties around where the lone breeze is blowing.

Gentle maid, you are fair and your tender glance is beaming ;
And your smile is as bright as the noon ;
And your sweet eyes are sad with the love-light that is gleaming,
As you dwell upon the tones of my tune.
Fair are the daughters of the Drinan Dun !
Dim be their splendors before thy sun!
Oh, my joy of Paradise ! I love thee out of measure ;
My soul thrills to thee in the pulsing of its pleasure.

Breathing silent beyond, where no mortal yet has wandered.
Are the banks strewn with dayesie and thyme ;
Where thy heart shall rejoice o'er the beauties thou hast pondered
In the visions of the bright young time.
Enter, my love, to the land of Maeve ! *
Where the rose bends, and the pansies wave ;
Where the little fairies, hiding thro' the tempest of the flowers,
Shyly glance as they sing, "Will you come to the bowers ?"

A FRAGMENT.

1881.

THE SAILING OF THE "EREBUS" AND "TERROR." PART OF AN
UNFINISHED POEM ON THE RETREAT OF FRANKLIN'S MEN TO-
WARDS THE GREAT FISH RIVER.

Now deeper the hollows that slumbering pour,
To wander and fade with a desolate roar ;
Night swims into morning, nor change to the view
Save washing Immensity's plunging renew —
With nought but the vast clouds above, where the sky
Grows dim as its change at each setting is nigh —
Save chance, 'mid the glare of its fearful surrender,
Down goes the big sun in a burst of red splendor,
And sheds its last gleams o'er the petrels in motion,
That circle like witches, and dance o'er the ocean;
While near, the wan sea-gull looks scornfully down,
And screams o'er the waters that hunger and drown,
With lengthy uprisings, where thunders appal
In storm-hills that heave with a bellowing fall.

---

* Maeve, Queen of the Irish Fairies, corrupted, by the English Spenser, into Mab.

ON THE AUGURS OF SCIENTIFIC NIHILISM.

1881.

LIKEWISE PART OF "FRANKLIN'S MEN," ETC.

Arch-curs of weak Science! though changed, yet the same,
That quenched in its pow'r the poor vanishing flame
Of pale Galileo — while broken and dying
The worn life exhausted, was ebbing and flying ;
And dawning looked sad on the sight that was dreaming,
While shone the lone truth from the mind that was teeming —
The track of lone grief on his face was engraven
While, staring to death, he passed under the raven.
" I've heard the town clock give its usual warning ;
I sleep but you'll waken my soul in the morning" — *
The morning has come ; and, through mists far dissolving,
The big world, half blind, from the past is revolving.

THE FIFTH OF NOVEMBER, 1854

WRITTEN AT SEVENTEEN.

It was dark upon the shores of the lonely Chersonese,
And the wind in gusty roars swayed the voices of the trees;
While the death of Autumn fell
                                        On the bloom ;
Ere the weary night had run, there the sentry on his gun
Stared and shuddered through the dun,
                                        Dreary gloom.

Darker shall that morn arise, fiercer shall the tempest rule,
Dreadful, in the dark surprise from the dim Sevastopool;
Hear they not the brazen chimes
                                        Distant toll ?
Nor the hum of rising life, with the sound of masses rife,
From that place of blood and strife,
                                        Muffling roll ?

---

*From "Ta me ma codlas na duze me" — *I am asleep, don't waken me.* This is the most weird and fearful song in existence. Its chorus runs like a chorus of dead men :

> " Mould candles in rows as they stood a-watching me,
> Mould candles in rows as they stood a-watching me,
> Cold in my coffin at the dawning of day."

The tune is wild and sweet, a heavy minor. My father sang it very often—so often in fact that the Droeshout face of the bard is always that which lies silent under the candles' glare. I have used the tune, in my illustration of the " Raven," as the " melancholy burden" of Poe's " Unhappy Master."

NOTE.—Truth is poetry in disguise. Our past stays where it began *to be.* *The world revolves* and the past is *left behind* even as *light* is. Our past stretches for countless *trillions* of miles, through the ocean of space ; our thoughts imprisoned in its omnipresent light. Its shape is tubular.

A faint and moving mass, shadowed by the mist and rain,
With their cannons slowly pass o'er the dark Tchernaya's plain:
And their numbers on the march
                              Dull the ground;
While the breathing from their coats, as it leaves their muffled throats
Sinks in vapor while it floats
                              Pale around.

Levies of the mighty Czar ! — and his mandate whirling forth,
Heaves the multitude afar unto Sibir of the North;
Trembling where Muskowa's tow'rs
                              Strange and old—
Dials of that misty clime, childish in a borrowed prime,
Pointing to the backward time, —
                              Glare in gold.

And hark, a smothered cry! and their pallid front is seen,
While the war-cloud sweeps on high through the mists that intervene,
And the shouting hills resound
                              To the plain;
While the cannon's grumble wells o'er the vaulting of the shells,
As for mastery, their yells
                              Rise amain.

Now in billows on the height, upwards in a boundless tide,
Come the rollings of the fight, bubbling from each moving side;
Fifteen thousand against three,
                              Drowning swarm;
And the flashing crowds prevailed, like a barrier assailed,
Where the dark horizons wailed
                              In the storm.*

Plunged beneath the living wave, spreading to the tempest nigh,
Mounting, with a sunken rave, thunders Britain's battle cry ;
Then gasped the burly Sclav's
                              Rattling breath,
As, mid struggle's wrench and pull, down he fell with bloody skull,
Ere he frowned and sunk in dull
                              Ashy death.

Hurled in slaughter from the slope yet unconquered, Russia's men
Strengthened, in a wider scope cloud the ledges once again :
Pouring with a mournful hymn
                              Like a dirge,
Which repeated in its cries, echoed gloomy to the skies
Like the winter sob that flies
                              Oe'r the surge.

*The "dark horizons" is a phrase used for that sublime spectacle sometimes perceived when sky and ocean appear to reel, and the lightnings line the *everywhere* with horizons. The Russians, later, numbered forty thousand, with sixty thousand in reserve.

Hear them with religious zeal chaunting for the Holy Czar!
Blazing in a waste of steel, wrathful in the strength of war;
While near their death alarum
                              Loud prolongs——
By the " Quarries " picket fence, quick'ning oĕ'r each eminence,
Come their doubling, misty, dense,
                              Howling throngs.

Hemmed on every side of flame, rooted with a frozen stare,
Stubborn, as the guns acclaim rained in murder through the air;
Now, 'gainst ten to one our lines
                              Moving, cheer ;
Higher still, as roaring loud, pressing thro' the battling crowd,
Nods the bearskin, sways the proud
                              Fusileer.

Upwards in eternal flow, rabid in their black designs;
Beaten, but to rise and show strange addition to their lines —
Onward ! still our soldiers cried,
                              And they run
Shouting in a hurried flock, as with clouds of battered rock
They defy the shotted lock
                              And the gun.

Vainly won! yet to the foes sang their Busby's* in the storm,
Frowzing horror where they close, and, as metal bent, re-form;
While their bay'nets once again
                              Glistened red
Thro' the human barricade, as they plied their bloody trade
And a scattered rampart made
                              Of the dead.

" Cathcart's fallen !" and the tale mutters fierce along the spurs,
Mingling with a vengeful wail, and the slogan's warring burrs;
" Faug a ballagh!" hear it sound
                              O'er the groans,
As with England's cry it runs, in a voice that rolling, stuns,
Where it storms above the gun's
                              Monotones.

Strange it broke upon the ear ! little knew the Russians then
Of that wild, appalling cheer.   Ah ! they heard it yet again,
And darkly, in the trenches
                              Rising swell;
Thro' the mournful mist it fled, high with slaughter wide and dread,
As it shook the night, and spread
                              Like a knell.

---
*"Busby" is the huge bearskin hat so often associated with Wellington's soldiers and Napoleon's " Old Guard."

Sons of poor old Erin's land! There 'twas Brian's battle song
Roused the valor, burning grand through the reign of crime and
   wrong ;
See them smiling where the shell's
       Humming, tune!
Scornful in a high renown—stormy to the battle's frown
Where the sun of blood went down
       In a swoon.

Hark! the jovial sons of France—and that moment sweeping past,
Came their colors in advance, to the warring trumpet's blast ;
Brightly now their bay'nets shine
       In the van,
And the " pas de charge " it hums o'er the loud "Avant!" that comes
'Mid the rollings and the drum's
       Rantan plan.*

Heroes, where the bravest fought, fiercely grand along the field;
Yet their daring might was nought, where the foeman still could wield
Thousands, fresh for blood and blows,
       On the plain—
Yet the crashing war confounds where the Russians lie in mounds,
And the bursting bomb rebounds
       'Mong the slain.

Stark and rigid crouch the dead, glaring darkly to the past;
Seeming, though the light were fled, each lone visage still was cast
On *him*, the coward robber
       Of his life;
Caesar o' the dainty curl, smiling, where the simple churl
Marched to death and giddying whirl
       'Mid the strife!

Ne'er again his native hill lights him with an humble joy ;
Nor the foolish mother's thrill greets the blushing soldier boy;
Unknown, he sinks in battle's
       Plunging hell,
Where the cannons rumbling, sound, as they plough the furrowed
   ground
With a blasting storm of round
       Shot and shell.

Sing the windy battle's roar! Oh! the horrors and the scenes,
Where the mangled Russians pour, crowding through the wet ravines;
" Huzza! huzza !! "—with, "O God
       Save us all!"——
Buried in a dreadful sleet, marching densely in retreat,
Now their faint and moving feet
       Rise and fall.

---

* Sometimes, with less euphony and correctness, called *rataplan*.

Heroes of the "Soldier's Fight!" Sound their glories thro' the world!
E'er in battle for the right may their standards be unfurled;
And England will remember
Yet a span,
Erin's sons who fought and led 'midst the dying and the dead,
On the stormy slopes of red
Inkermann.

A REVIEW.

Putnam & Sons: 2 Vo.—*The Noble Art of Bawding*. We have just received the twentieth edition of this book, and after a lengthened survey of its contents we must confess that, though the subject is handled in a masterly manner and runs through a matter of some eight or nine hundred pages, still, as we have heretofore mentioned, *hic blatherinorum ergo dam*, the book remains incomplete. Now while he has given us the addresses of all the *sporting* houses in town, he has, notwithstanding all his caution and erudition, not given us a single chapter touching the chances or opportunities of our *best* and *most exclusive* classes. Now there is not a single reporter on our staff, whose precarious living and uncertain items have made them considerably "up to snuff," who could not have told him that the hotel chambermaid and the needy shop-girl are easily cajoled under promise of marriage. Why, bless you, our streets are crowded since honor was declared of no service in this age of improvement—in fact the fashion of attending the levees of the cultured Cyprian is no longer in vogue with the *dilettante*. The professional bawd is in despair, for in order to compete with the new opposition she is compelled to become a waitress, or a school-girl with slate and satchel; and they have good cause to lament the present depression of the market. What with the latter in shop, kitchen and factory we may well look to the future with confidence; to the day when marriage is banished as a nuisance, and virtue becomes as cheap as mouldy hake. Already that tiresome and despotic tie has been relegated to the land of shadow—with the present condition of laws a man can shuffle off his wives and take to others as often as he chooses. In fact to be a bawdy-master now-a-days one should be always attended by a lawyer and a churchman—the one to marry him at night, the other to release him in the morning.

WE ARE ALL JOLLY FELLOWS THAT FOLLOW THE PLOUGH.

TUNE—My father's " We are all Jolly Fellows," etc., etc.

1883.

Sing a cheer for the lasses, ye blades bright and gay,
For the merry green stack and the plunge of the hay;
Where the Druids sang high, as they tript in their glee,
O we'll roll the glad chorus and hail the green tree.
Derry down, down; down derry down.*

Sing the brisk roundelay, for the harvest is nigh,
And we dance to the smile of the beautiful sky;
While we cheer to the lark, as it skims in the blue,
Ere it trills to our song with a fading adieu.
Derry down, down; down derry down.

Will you dance, my dim lassie? come blithely, my jo!
And we'll pledge the grand hope with a glass of stingo;
For the fairest rejoice with the sons of the flail,
And they'll toast to each kiss as we drain the brown ale.
Derry down, down; down derry down.

---

*The above chorus was that sung by the religious bards or Druids when dancing around the oak on which hung the sacred mistletoe.

Who would pine for worn pleasures midst pale damosels,
As they drawl their sick fancies where Love never dwells?
But the brown maids, more tender, will waste the sweet vow
On the brave jolly fellows that follow the plough.
Derry down, down; down derry down.

Will you tie up my bonnet?   Pray, turn thy bright eyes!
Let us kiss for sweet cherries—and gaily we rise;
While we shake the green boughs as we turn in the ring,
And we kiss 'neath the arch, while we merrily sing:
Derry down, down; down derry down.

From the cool jugs, half-brimming, all fresh, sweet and pure,
We will pour the new milk by the hedge-keeper's door;
Where the sunny girl smiles as she ravels the skein,
And the blue-bottle jigs as he hums on the pane.
Derry down, down; down derry down.

When at last we return, in the blaze of the moon,
O what sly stolen kisses! what hearts all in tune!
While the shy lasses press us, and sweetly avow
That we're all jolly fellows that follow the plough.
Derry down, down; down derry down.

O my heart's in the daisies where'er I may roam;
So I'll toast a fond glass to the mem'ries of home;
Tho' the stranger may sneer, and the cold winters blow,
Yet I'll swell the glad song of the sweet long ago,
With my *Down, down; down derry down.*

THE SONG OF THE JUNE MEADOWS.

A COMPANION TO THE "SONG OF THE HAYMAKERS."

1881.

The dead summer glows, and we trample the hay,
As we toil in the waning of June;
And the hot steel burns as it swings in its play
To the song of the reapers in tune;
The waggoner warbles his low, drowsy song
As his cart rumbles faint to the load;
Turning far from the town, while the grass trails down
As he fades in the dust of the road.
See the blue rays dance where the corn-field waves,
As it bursts in its wide hymn of praise;
And the meadow's breath swoons, as it sinks 'mid the noons
Of the bright-burning, midsummer days.

Chorus:—

> Then a song and a cheer for the bonny green stack,
>   Climbing up to the sun warm and high;
> For the pitchers, the rakers, and the merry haymakers,
>   And the beautiful midsummer sky.

The wild posy blows where the buttercups reign,
    And the honey bee winds o'er the frond;
And the pale blossom sighs to the swell of the grain
    Flaring gold to the cowslips beyond;
Jocund, o'er the sward, comes the fat, rosy throng,
    Stained with red berries plucked in the maze;
And the sunny light gleams, while they frolic in its beams,
    As they cheer through the mist of its rays;
'Mong the rich perfume, Jennie waits by the hedge,
    While her sweet bonnet turns in the sun;
Peeping, bashful and dim, thro' the flow'rs on its rim,
    As she turns where their day's work is done.

> Then a song and a cheer, etc., etc.

When each hue fades low where the pale cot smiles,
    And the young chirp sinks in the drone,*
And the red sky smoulders afar in its isles,
    There she stands by the gate all alone ;
Sweet as the honeysuckle climbing the wall,
    She's the pride of the poor and the old ;
While the warm shadows dwell as she dips from the well,
    Where the beams on the worn shoes unfold :
Lowly she speaks, as she points him the way,
    As soft as a vision in her bloom ;
And she smiles in his sight thro' the dim lovely light,
    While he sighs as he wends through the gloom.

> Then a song and a cheer, etc., etc.

---

* The drone of dying day; the hum of lessening toil.

DEATH CHAUNT OF A CONDEMNED MURDERER.

1880.

The succeeding lament is founded upon five lines of my father's terrible original "Lament of Jonathan Heywood," a murderer who was hung in the front of Kirkdale jail in 1857. Never shall I forget the way in which my father sang his dreadful chaunt—a tune that he composed. Entering by sympathy into every condition and situation of human life (for his mind was complete and rounded in every department), he did not sing as it were, but stirred the air with a sort of soundless emotion. Nothing appeared but horror, grief, and dread-sounding wails, shuddering and thickening around, until the listener was drawn into an absolute ocean of emotion, from which he never totally emerged. He was the discoverer of human heart-strings, and has left in the writer's memory the heirloom of some thousands of tunes—a great many of which are his own, and some, the products of his ancestor, Turlough. The remains of my father's original are found, slightly altered, in the two lines that terminate the second and third stanzas with the last line of the fourth stanza—five lines in all.

The gloom of midnight sets around me ; my light is waning low
    and pale;
And longer drums the watch-tow'r's warning amidst the shadows of
    the jail;
No tears can dry my bursting anguish, nor ban this dark and dis-
    mal cell;
My strong-bound arms are wet with sorrows that mortal tongue can
    never tell.

These iron doors—avaunt, false terror ! 'tis but a foul and change-
    ful dream;
O God ! that I should here invoke Thee, or gaze upon the fearful
    beam:
How can I ever hope for pardon—the thought is dreadful to me
    now—
When at the bar of Boundless Justice, with MURDER stamped
    upon my brow !

Methinks I see my murdered victim, where voiceless death upon
    him lay,
And in his parting stare the meeting that cries upon the Judgment
    Day ;
In dreams I see the fatal finger that points unto his bloody
    tomb,
And hear him cry with shrieks of horror, " Prepare, prepare to
    meet your doom ! "

How long my worn and fevered fancy shall hear the ceaseless, tol-
    ling bell
That drowns the death-pulsating hammer, like a fitful sounding
    knell !
I see the scaffold, darkly rising, above the surge of faces round—
The clock strikes twelve—my life is ending !—my blood runs cold
    to hear the sound !

At sunset hour my case was rendered ; my brother did my hopes
 deny,
And on the book he swore against me, amidst the great crowd's
 listening cry ;
The fire above the sash declining, upon his out-stretched arm did
 fall,
And as I turned in hounded sorrow—a gallows danced upon the
 wall !

'Twas drunken frenzy, deaf to mercy, that urged my passions
 hoarsely on,
And stirred me with the shout of " Murder !" above the voice of
 senses gone ;
My grief arose with wailing shudder ; I stared—O Christ, the deed
 was done !
I fled ; and now my time is closing, my days are spent, my race
 is run.

Oh, cursed night ! slow-dragging wain, that hails to the grey dawn
 faint and dim ;
Meet hearse to greet the moody hangman, with patient silence cold
 and grim ;
Black mournful shroud ! your end shall waken with yawning crowds
 and drunken boys,
Where long eternity shall swoon, ere falls the trap with a rattling
 noise.

Adieu, the careless world that slumbers, unmindful of the coming
 morn ;
Bereft of life while life is pleasing, I go to meet a death of scorn ;
Of what the future path may lead to, alas ! but senseless words are
 known;
The grim road points in silent anguish, and wends in shadows dark
 and lone.

Adieu to thee ! the dearest vision of years that throb with grief
 and pain;
Fit shade unto this dreadful dawning, the years I've sought your
 face in vain;
My name, upheld to execration, in crime's dead flood shall sink and
 drown;
Till nought shall tell my mournful end, save the *blood-red stain*
 within the town.

66

THE BARD'S REVERIE.

Dec., 1883.

The silver blows upon the air, the trees are stirred with harmony ;
Come listen to my melody
　　　　And tend upon my pleasant rune;
The glowing mists in fairy rings float o'er the mere with thrilling
　　　　wings,
And every star in Aiden sings
　　　　Around the giddy moon.

The golden lake is burning green, come sail beyond the steps of
　　　　pearl ;
Nor tarry long, my queenly girl,
　　　　The purple night will soon be gone !
And we will troll by Maeva's side, where chaunting fishes plunge
　　　　and glide,
And burning fins illume the tide,
　　　　In courses trembling on.

Below the land that angels know, where Summer sings and flow'rets
　　　　bloom.
That lies beyond the merry tomb
　　　　Below the realm of Emminee;
Beneath this lake, upon the shore, where Sorrow sits forevermore;
I spy, amidst the living roar,
　　　　A tuneless Memorie.

Then let us haste, O haste to night ! and wake his harp with tones
　　　　of love,
And point him to the joys above;
　　　　Nor scorn the lowly son of song;
For high into the burning road, there's ne'er a toiler that has trod,
But finds within the Arch of God
　　　　A thrill to him belong.

SIR HUSSAY'S ADDRESS TO ROSA JUNE.

1882.

Come list the nobler strain! with heart renewed in pain,
I turn from faces rosy, sweet and jolly;
Source of my hope and care! why blooms the world so fair,
And thrills my soul in tender melancholy?

Turn, lady, sweet and coy, my sun, my golden joy !
Last of my dreams ! in brimming love I fear thee;
Last of the good and true ! my hopeful dreams renew;
My soul is sunless, save when I am near thee.

Where floats, beyond the tomb, 'mid sighs of precious bloom,
The muse of drowsy meadows soft and glowing;
Where Beauty, blazing grand, smiles in the summer land,
We'll roam, where jocund streams beyond are flowing.

There steal the noon-day hours thro' mists of juicy flow'rs,
And nodding blue-bells to the bees are rhyming;
And by the water's brim, the jasper billows swim,
As on the beach the golden shells are chiming.

High in the sphere of Cause, we'll scorn the coward's laws,
And proudly own sweet Nature in our glances —
Free, in a gentle sway, to love, but not obey;
While nobler freedom with thy love advances.

Where golden Time shall swim through Progress vast and dim,
Lost in thy soul, and with thy spirit blending,
We'll smile amid the morn of cycles yet unborn,
United, and eternally ascending.

DESMOND'S LOVELY VALLEYS.

1881.

Far through the blazing light rode helm and corselet bright,
    As Coulin through the Saxon Pale was turning;
His flashing targe it rung, and from his shoulders hung
    The saffron hues of Erin, fiercely burning.

Among the lonesome hills, where yell a thousand rills,
    Where silent cliffs call backward as he sallies,
Ringing the mossy world from ruined mountains hurled,
    He sweeps along through Desmond's lovely valleys.

Where frowns the castle high, in menace to the sky,—
    Where on its walls a bloody head is staring,—
He sings of Mary's charms, and through the quick alarms,
    He bears in might the loveliest foe of Airinn.

Scarcely the warder knew his fierce "Lammh dearg aboo,"*
    When past the bridge the Saxon horse is foaming,
And o'er the distant vale pursue the wild Owneyl;
    But sank their toiling steeds amid the gloaming.

"Sweet maid, mine only love! I swear by her above,
    The moon, that rolls in splendor by the mountains,
Far from a world of care, a rosy path we'll share,
    Where Paradise descends amid the fountains."

---

* The war-cry of the O'Neill—" Red Hand Forever."

"Thou art my pride," she said, and hung her blushing head;
   He kissed her loving eyes at fondest leisure,
So tender in his sight, while shone the mellow light,
   For dainty love, her sweetness, and his pleasure.

Unto the moonlit air he sang her beauty fair;
   In drowsy joy she chid his fancies glowing;
He kissed her once again, while faintly in its strain
   The dying strings in tuneful sighs were blowing.

Against the silver moon, while 'neath with roses strewn,
   His charger to the harp in silence rallies;
Till, slower through the wild, where dreamy grandeur smiled,
   They slept and rode through Desmond's lovely valleys.

"QUOTH THE RAVEN, 'NEVERMORE.'"

I think Poe (if we may make a doubtful exception in the case of James Clarence Mangan) was the greatest *poet* that ever this world has seen. As a poet, pure and simple, he stands unrivalled. His lines are melodies. Shakspeare and the rest are *creators;* as *poets* they were full of flaws. I love the rugged creators; their over-powering genius thrills me; but poetry—it is a lost emotion, gone, gone from earth. Among the Irish bards all poems were recited to the chaunt of thrumming harps. Poems were songs in monotone. It is but just to say that Poe, whose ancestors were from "green Erin of the streams," should think as the bards did, and advocate sweetness of rhyme as one of the main elements of poetry. America has produced only one great poet—Poe, the genius who was too great to be comprehended save by man at his tenderest and best.

Concerning the "Raven," I have been "dreaming dreams no mortal ever dared to dream before." As well as Doré, I have illustrated the "Raven." Our ideas are as wide as the poles. Doré's are beautiful; there is a tranquil loveliness in them unusual to Doré. Mine are stormier, wilder and more weird; they are more horrible; I have reproduced mentality and phantasm. Not one of the ideas were ever drawn before. I feel that Poe would have said that I had been faithful to *his* idea of the "Raven," for I have followed his meaning so close as to be merged into his individuality. I have not finished the series yet, but when I do, it will be more numerous than Doré's.

A DREAM OF FLORIDA.

A SEAMAN'S "SHANTY," OR CHORUS SONG.

Floridian skies! shine on my sails,—
Aho! you land of flowers—
And waft me far to St. John river,
Where oft I've whiled the sunny hours.
For near its banks a lady dwells,—
Away! you breezes blowing—
Upon a beach of golden shells,
O yoe! come, cheery! I'm bound away.

Then sweetly blow ye noonday winds,
And waft me far to St. John river;
There's lots of gold, for rovers bold,
On the shores of Eldorado!

I know a place on St. John River;—
Aho! you breezes blowing,—
Where posies nod their honey'd stores
And sun-rain on the wave is flowing.
Then stir my shrouds, you dwelling gales!
Aho! bright fans of summer;
And breathe your peace upon my sails,
O yoe! come cheery! I'm bound away.

Then sweetly blow, ye noonday winds,
And waft me far to St. John River;
There's lots of gold, for rovers bold,
On the shores of Eldorado!

BE OF HOPE! BE OF HOPE!

1883.

This appeal is the composition of my brother William. It is founded on the title of a lost song of my father's that was suppressed by the government. England has literally extirpated the higher poesy of Erin; nothing remains (save a few isolated glories that have survived the buffetings of neglect and tyranny) but the commonplace ditties of such little Saxoneens and mediocres as Moore and his followers. But happily the sons of the bards are yet in Erin—the unsuppressed enthusiasm is handed down, and while the tunes remain, the spirit of the lost effusions shall sound forth with redoubled volume and power.

By the mem'ry of the dead, be of hope! be of hope!
And our martyrs that have bled, Sons of Erin be of hope!
By the gibbet, axe and wheel, and the headsman's bloody steel—
By the glories of O'Niell, Sons of Grannia be of hope!

By the mem'ry of the past, be of hope! be of hope!
And the battle's furious blast, Sons of Erin be of hope!
By Blackwater's famous fight, by Benburb and Owen's might,
And the "Sun-burst' waving bright, Sons of Grannia be of hope!

Oh, by Sarsfield's gleaming blade, be of hope! be of hope!
And the shout of Clare's Brigade, Sons of Erin be of hope!—
When the cheers of Fontenoy, rolled on Flanders fierce and high,
Then the Saxon knew the cry, Sons of Grannia be of hope!

In the dungeon dark and drear, be of hope! be of hope!
Scorn the voice of death and fear, Sons of Erin be of hope!
For there dawns a brighter day when these dastards we'll repay,
Then be patient for the fray, Sons of Grannia be of hope!

1877.

MY GREEN LAND IERNIE.

When *Eirinn* was young, and her bright sun was beaming,
Ere Teamor's gray walls through her twilight lay dreaming,
The green silken folds in their glories were streaming
  To the harp's lulling tones in the land of sweet reveries.
The stranger was welcomed; her heart was out-poured,
With the feast of her mind and the wealth of her board;
And the Saxon* rejoiced in the Halls of the Sword—
But the nod of weak Rome, o'er that kind heart so tender,
Wrought the foul deed of tears that no Saxon could render,
As she bowed o'er the sword that could bravely defend her—
  And such was the fall of my green land Iernie.

Nor tarnished she rose by each fool dim and hoary,
When Brian the Brave carved a name in her story;
Nor shadowed was Malachy's sword in his glory
  When the standards of Woden slept under the raven;
When Thor's bloody heroes like stubble went down
'Neath the war-crash of shields in their battled renown;
Our stormy Dalcassians cleft high to the frown
Of the death-grinning Danes, by Deblana's red water;
While laughed the wild North to the sound of the slaughter—
Ere the Saxon was leagued with false Dairmid's pale daughter,
  And the bards in lament woke the glens of Iernie.

Green land of the streams! though the traitor has bound thee,
And cowards disown ye, the Future's have crowned thee;
Though bright by thy robes when the greater surround thee,
  Accept the rude strains of the last of thy minstrels!
Kind *Eirinn a-ruin!* O, my glad spirit sings
As I bend in thy shades o'er the lone, humming strings;
For the dawn soon shall rise o'er the night's tardy wings,
And I sound its grand tones as in darkness I ponder;
My heart's pulse to thee! Oh, where'er I may wander,
Sweet land of my fathers! as proud, aye, and fonder,
  I'll thrum for thy freedom, my green land Iernie.

---

*Alfred the Great received his education in Erin, and thus, indirectly, Ireland bestowed on the Saxons what *their* descendents refused to the Irish. In reference to Rome I would state that it was by a *bull* that the Irish were ‘led by tho horns." The Irish chieftains swore fealty to the English monarch, because Breakspeare (the first and only English Pope) commissioned that monarch to, as it afterwards proved, enslave the Irish.

NOTE.—Pronounce the above name I-air-nee.

Erin's Black Sorrow.—A Lament.

Battle March of the Kernes.*

*The Hy Niall and Dalcassian armies marched into battle to the fluttering strains of harps and chaunters, which soothed the chafing spirits of these saffron-shirted warriors, and made their advance the most imposing and majestic, as well as the most terrible, in the world.

Tyrone of the Glories.

Marching song.   *Brass, fifes and drums.*

Plaint of Rosaline.

Death Chaunt of a Condemned Murderer.*

*The above chaunt is not the composition of the writer, but of the writer's father.

Burial of Owen Roe.*

*Owen Roe O'Neill, a prince of Ulster; the victor of Benburb. Owen, had he lived, would have crossed swords with Cromwell, but the Cromwellians poisoned "him, whom they feared to meet with steel."

Sweet Friends, your Love and Health I Pledge! The Brimming Glass we'll Drain!

NOTE.—The above tune "Sweet Friends, Your Love and Health I Pledge! The Brimming Glass we'll Drain," was composed by the writer at four years of age. It was founded on my father's "Oh, why did I Desert?"—the same tune as the "Boughel Roe." I sang it to my father, and he was so pleased with its pathos that he sang his "Deserter" to this tune during the remaining years of his life.

Out of the hundreds composed by the writer, the preceding tunes are the average representative, I put in what is nearest to hand. Most of the tunes are in simple melody —the harmony or "padding" he leaves to others. Pure melody or tune is the test of the composer; the *soul* of a composition is in the barren and naked *strength* of a tune. For this reason the writer prefers the Bards to Mozart, Beethoven or Handel. The latter was truly enlightened when he said that he preferred the simple strains of "Eileen Aroon" (Anglicised under the name of "Robin Adair") to his own cherished and ambitious effusions. The creation of a great tune is the creation of a great poem. What must we think of the sublime genius who composed "Savourneen Deelish" ("Exile of Erin")? Not all the symphonies of the Germans can compare with the strains of the Bards—and why? Because harmony, so necessary to the rendition of tune, is the mechanical and inferior branch of minstrelsy—it is the necessary "filling in" that can be done by ordinary minds under the stimulus of severe education. How many thousands of air-shuddering harmonies have I heard since I was breeched?—how many good tunes?—*not one.* I do not dispraise the thickening of tunes by varying and interblending strains, for it is absolutely *necessary*; I shall employ it hereafter *in hurricanes*—but I shall hold all valueless if the *foundation* is not made of the pure gold of melody. Let "Savourneen Deelish" be thickened like Mendelssohn's "Wedding March," and compare the two! The latter has no *particular* meaning, whereas the first tells, in every measure, the profound yet melting tenderness of a generous sorrow. Composers do not put *kindness* into their songs; the quality is rare. Most songs, to the writer, *make fun* of themselves. For instance, one bar is a laugh, another a groan, another the cry of a forlorn Chinese goose—and all, together, palmed off as a love song! Music, like poetry, is a mass of *linked* emotions, and none but those who feel and express *terrific* emotion will ever live in the hearts of enlightened ages. The writer is the first who has ever hinted concerning the correctness of music; as for the *art* of music, it has *practically* no existence. It takes as much brains to be a composer as to be a poet, for a knowledge of *mind* is necessary. For this reason a complete and rounded mind can only hope to succeed in real music; hence the claim of the complete Bard requires a name that is greater than anything that music, philosophy, the drama, poetry or painting as yet furnishes—five Shakspeares in one.

Be of Hope! Be of Hope!

The end of the above measure
greatly prolonged and droned.

LOVE.

There is not one in a thousand who comprehends love in its intellectual reach. Love is a reality; man makes of it an unreality. Millions of huddling fools, flung together, build millions of paradises on the strength of a mere sensation, fancying themselves lovers, when they are the dupes of a cynical Nature which gulls their senses with aerial fantasies, making slaves of boors under the mirage of choice and free will. Once satiated, their love is tossed to the dogs. They have bred their kind, and Nature is done with them. Tut! they but prove to the philosopher that Nature has higher reward, and makes fools only of dupes and sensualists.

The basis of love, of all loves, is selfishness. Prate as we may, we love only that which gives *us* pleasure. He who is *perfectly* selfish seeks the love, the respect, and the admiration of all.

Since Propagation is the *main* end of Nature, treating the love after its accomplishment as unworthy of respect or preservation, it becomes the duty of the watchful few to preserve the latter by substitution of a different law, thereby flourishing their defiance against its brutalizing lower tendencies. We must substitute it by a *higher* Nature; the Nature we know, and which comes with a conquering front at our command.

Everything associated with love as at present understood, must be held contemptuously in the back ground. To make love stand the test of reason, we must begin by first *using* our reason.

You must analyze the condition of your opposites. Look at them as *men*, and see whether, as men, you would turn to them as the dearest friends on earth. Comradeship is what you must behold in your opposite; companionship in your mental and moral life. To marry a mental inferior is harlotry, and bastards, not true-born children, are the

result. Woman is said to be man's equal in general, since she culti-
vates a different portion of the brain. Time however will tell.

Children must not enter into the calculations of the true lover until he understands the laws. If he desires children, let him see that
conditions are present for the evolution of a *true representative;* otherwise he is cursed with an aborted and diminished image, the reward
of his own criminality. Were law and not lust the rule, every child by
the combination of two opposite natures would surpass its parents.
Think, then, on the barbarism of this self-punishing age!

By first beginning with judgment, we end with perfect love. Mind
is the savior and director of the affections.

Some will say that this would end half the love in existence; that
criticism would "brush the dew from the rose" — and so on. But let
them remember that that which will not stand the test of criticism is, in
itself, unreal and metaphysical.* To a nature that can *love*, the test of
criticism but gives greater confidence. Truth can stand the sun, only
the false would bar the light. Love must be a vasty luxury and com-
modious to the crowds when sensualists own to it, and silly girls become its advocates! What is there in either of them to love, to waste
a thought on, or to cast an eye! Every fool wants an ideal—what then
does he furnish?

Depend upon it, that love is rarer than the Aurora; the prize of
the unselfish alone. Only the loving can love, only the gentle and true.

THE DIGNITY OF MAN.

1881.

What is a gentleman? Tut, says the world, it is a common thing.
Anybody that is well-dressed and frozen, with manners taken from a
book of etiquette, can pass off in society as a gentleman. Some of
these without the least notion of *unwritten* gentility, imagine themselves superior beings, and will sit down and survey the rest of mankind with a cold and automatic stare. So strange an influence do they
unconsciously wield that their betters, the less ignorant, feel at times
pervaded by their "dignity," and, from want of thought, attribute it to
the presence of *something* superior. That superiority, however, is nothing but the sublimated essence of self-esteem continually thrown off by
these diminished individuals — poor ornaments that make the ignorant
bow without either knowing the wherefore or the why.

Nature in making a fool (a product which, without cynicism, I
may honestly say occupies her mostly at present), to save him from the
abasement and degradation which must naturally ensue to the condition, oftentimes creates him with a tremendous swelling of self-esteem,
bulging his poll like a camel's hump and slanting his front like the
bows of a Portugeuse lurcher. That this is a wise ordination I cannot

---

*Nothing but a lie is ever "too sacred" for complete, exhaustive, *scornful* and *scorching*
investigation. To repel the scorner without *proof on hand* is a secret admission of groundless
assumption.

but wish to believe, for self-respect is the key to a higer progression. It is not against pride that I would inveigh; pride is as great a quality as any in the calendar. The trouble, however, commences when Nothing becomes proud in the presence of Something; thereby ignoring the truth of progression. The superior becomes debased by the *pretension* of the inferior, and sinks from lack of a truer self-knowledge.

The first question that becomes necessary in order to know the difference should be at once propounded. This is momentous, and should be the judicial soliloquy of every person in the land. *Am I a fool, or not?* No fool can be a gentleman. In order to know whether fate has placed *Fool!* on your cranium or not, it behooves you to know this fact, and to ponder it well. There are but two classes among the people, creators, and non-creators or gatherers of material. These two classes create a medium or go-between class—creator-gatherers. If you cannot create in the arts or sciences, you are a gatherer or fool, and your place is marked down.* Though you have *gathered* enough money from your fellow men to set the world staring for a year, you are still but a gatherer, for, neither *creating* nor *earning* it (for no man can *earn* a million), you are no better than a brick gatherer, with this difference, you are dishonest. To call all millionaires *thieves*, shall be reserved for a more enlightened age.

But the creator, being the gentleman, must not be a liar. Truth is the handmaid of true gentility. You must also be a creator of new facts, not a gatherer of old ones. A mere writer of stale things, under this head, would be a gatherer or fool, while an original shoemaker would be a gentleman. To be a truthful creator, however, the truth must be known.

What is truth? Truth is the incontradictible. What is that which cannot be contradicted? *Contradiction itself.*† In other words, truth is the *simultaneous* perception of *both* sides of a question—a thing that can only be done by those who think *in masses*, the most excitable people in the world. However, though the masses cannot think truly, since they are slow and hesitating, they can learn to think so by incessant practice; once knowing the truth they shall behold the superior animal, or gentleman. The first duty of gentlemen is to *learn* what is truth; the second, to *speak* it; the third, to *advance* it.

True greatness is producible, and gentility is portable property. A man whose greatness consists in owning acres and farms, ceases to be great in the truer sense, since he is great only by relation—he cannot carry his acres on his back. Money may be great, but it is great *in itself*, and cannot bestow greatness on its possessor. Nobility is *self-given*, and for a fool to attempt to bestow nobility is quite as laughable as the bestowal of brains by letters patent.

Yet upon this system and plan, what the world styles gentleman, has lorded it over his superiors by the mere possession of a greater

*The moral question requires the gentlemanly creator as well, for he who cannot create *new virtues* is a gatherer, and has no claim to the superior. Knowledge alone is virtue; knowledge of correct emotions—through lack of knowledge, of complete and rounded intellect, virtue becomes mere snobbery, worshipping the false—hence this is a world of barbarous snobs, male and female.

† That which is self-refuting is also self-asserting, for in telling us what it is not, it tells us by negation what it is. But facts will not search for us, we must search for them.

self-esteem; he *feels* greater, and, therefore, must perchance *be* greater.

And now, I would impress with almost stubborn solemnity, one fact upon the reader of these lines, viewing the future sublimity of progressive man. To whomsoever you act or speak (though it be to what the weak world has elevated to absolute godhood) let him be but a simple man; and if inferior to you in brains and benevolence, your natural servant and follower. Let this be a law to you in every day's practice, enclosed in your hearts and bound by rugged walls. Do this, and a high republicanism shall flourish, advancing beyond mere idle statutes and neglected laws.

"The fault lies not in our stars, but in *ourselves*, that we are underlings;" Coriolanus can live beneath a coat in rags, for the coat does not make the slave but the heart beneath it. A rigid soul can bend the creature of condition by the silent pressure of a prouder scorn; for the strength of *men* can shrink the pretensions of the titled pauper to an idle shadow. We have come into this world with our bodies free from clothes; what we may wear has been the thought of others—we care not who. Let us walk superior to the outer cover; to be a *man* in rags is a prouder boast than to be descended from a line of kings. A thousand years of consecrated scrofula may holloa its parting whispers of the divinity surrounding kings; but we can boast a prouder name, strong with the future's weal. There is a nobility in the name of man that makes contemptible the glitter of fools; with aspiration unclouded by the shows of fools, man towers too high to be royal—he is the god under whose shadow the insects crawl, playing at crowns and thrones.

A NOON-DAY DREAM.

The merry lark skims whistling in the sky,
The road is brown, and Summer stirs the breeze;
While in the noon the hay-stack waves on high;
And burrs the mead with drowsy humming bees.

All Nature beams, and Beauty glows around;
The sun-bright cups their tender hues unfold,
Fresh with a lucent green the hedge is drowned,
Where floats the blue-bird in a storm of gold.

The sleepy toad sits lonely in the gloom;
And high the clover swells in gentle sighs,
Spanning the field with dews of honey bloom;
While burnished clouds in torrid splendors rise.

Now by this gentle throne of jessamine
I scan the field in silent state obscure,
While at my feet the smiling flow'rs entwine,
Nor feel the sense that proudly scorns the poor.

The tender vales bring back the pleasing tears;
For oft I've rambled through the shady lane,
Ere laughter saddened with the silent years
That filled my heart with childish grief and pain.

Full oft in England's merry land I've gazed,
And plucked the primrose and the pansy blue;
And, where the green duck's neck in splendor blazed,
I've swelled my gladness to the cock's halloo,

You breathing groves, you joyous dells of song!
With fluttering tones and soft recording show'rs;
How can ye spread such trembling swells along,
With ceaseless warblings, through the burning hours?

See where the roving bloom delights the air,
With dewy pinions trembling in the wind,
With radiance thrilled, it dies in perfume rare,
And seeks expression in the poet's mind.

There shall it bloom in bow'rs that never fade,
And flush new changes thro' each deathless span;
There's ne'er a beauty by sweet Nature made
But finds its Eden in the soul of man.

Nor aye can blindness blur the dreamy fires
That blow senescent 'mid the storm of rules;
High shall the future swell with great desires,
And spurn the vain philosophy of tools.

For what can aid the vasty flight of thought,
But mounting war, that flings the stormy sage —
Tardy the wings by vaunt mechanics wrought,
The rusty motors of an iron age.

The wealth of halls, the wondrous waste of spires,
Swoon grimly down, the boast of sinking pride—
Curst are the treasures of our goodly sires
Uncoined of wealth we never can divide.

A fitful view is but the rich man's dow'r,
Faint be the sight and poor his blank reward;
True riches smile not in the miser's pow'r —
While all the Pleasures cheer the careless bard.

Far from the joyless splendors of the town
E'er could I rove, and pipe my sylvan glee,
Where cherries dance, and, o'er the woodland brown,
The gushing throats renew the sweet "pu-wee."

The cuckoo's note, the cat-bird's merry cry,
The dragon's wing that whirrs o'er brawling streams;
These are the sounds that trance the soulful eye,
Where sunbeams wander 'mid the poet's dreams.

PROMETHEUS—A CHAUNT OF THE RUDE.

Dec. 1883.

The world was dark; and great Prometheus chained;
Bound on a Scythian crag, a frightful ledge
That scowled its terrors o'er a blank abyss—
The swart abode and brooding place of storms:
A sunken frost slept in its voiceless deeps,
And silence slumbered in the yawn of air.

    *   *   *   *   *   *

His head was bowed, and on his cumbrous arms,
Strong-bound unto the wild and frozen crags,
Bit the rude irons to the central bone—
Thus prone he lay, the ruined hope of man—
Last of the Titan race by Jove abhorred.
The gods rejoiced, nor felt the heinous wrong;
The spawn of space, unfit to rule the world!
Nor judged the tyrants till the time drew nigh,
Man's scornful claim to hurl their bodies down
And batter their heads with thunders.
Prometheus turned, and mutely stared on high,
Searching the wandering clouds, the fitful sky,
Ashen with horror:
Yet spoke he not but hung his mournful head,
While woes Titanic shook his blasted frame;
And from his chest, pierced with an iron bar,
Out-gushed the swollen grief of his huge ribs
(Turned from his throat by Scorn's gigantic pow'r)
In bloody sobs, a steep and horrid drain:
And with each sob, while the rough chains did moan,
The strong hills shuddered to such voiceless groan.

    *   *   *   *   *   *

Now came the storms, the messengers of Jove,
Whose vengeful fires drowsed in the thickening clouds;
With shagged forms they rose from Tartarus,
And spread a bitter terror through the world.
Wan Scythia wailed with lamentation,
And the bear cowered with a frozen gasp—
Out from the desert roared a frightful peal,
And sudden blackness shuddered through the air:
Rocked the lone hills, whose wedgéd cataracts,
Torn from the granite's top, ran staggering down,
Till, in the sweep and whirl of boisterous winds
The mountains wandered—howling through the plains.
The sky's hoarse rage with mingling clamors flung
(Bowling in thunders) the grim lightnings,
Death's hurrying messengers, clothed in wrath.
Against the hills their war-dints clamoréd,
Frighting the rock-shades, the cold serpents dim,

With hissing slaughter; then, with railing clouds,
Burst fearful on the strong tempestuous front
Of huge Prometheus, the Immortal Sage,
Locking his head amidst the grinning crags,
Ploughing his body up, and's mighty limbs
Riving with coward pangs —the dastard might,
Torn from old Saturn, of presumptuous Jove—
Well might the hated monster swell with joy,
And vaunt his wisdom from lascivious beds,
Whiles from the crags he heard the direful storm
That poured with ruin on the Friend of Man!
Nor yet Prometheus moaned, but with a scorn
Out of all span, stared widely to the skies,
And his big wounds gave forth the muttered change
That swells portentous from the dying swan—
Ee'n while the ocean, torn and beaten down
Before the storms which thrashed the clouds to flames,
Lifted its boundless stretch in horrible waves,
Cloud-dark'ning heads that shook with drowning roars;
And raving scornful o'er the storm's dread wars,
Drenched in wild thunders to the vaulting stars

*   *   *   *   *   *

Through the swart blankness of thick-stunnéd Night,
Death's cloudy witch and Hell's own paramour,
O'er breathless wastes, athwart the rattling clouds,
Rode the lone wing, screaming—
Fierce kinsman to the bird of throbbing eyes,
The haggard raven: His hard beak did slant
The quickening hues that stung the drunken clouds
To reeling thunders; and the air he clave
With archéd grandeur—'twas the bird of Jove:
Dark, in the tempest, tossed his royal wings,
Clouding the air, and fearfully raving;
His curving scythe keen with an edge of death:
Over Prometheus stirred his monstrous plumes
Shaking with carnage; and his brownéd crest,
Stained with the reek and bloody drench of wars,
Lifted with menace, while each feather rose
Horridly fluttering; then from his throat,
E'en while his curtain'd eyes rang dreadly down,
Arose a sound so thick and harsh with rage,
Of such long-drawn and hoarse destruction,
Like that which gasps from the half-smothered floe,
That the wide frost bellowed; railing mistily,
Till silence shivered, and brooded echoless.
Another came, and the hills answeréd,
Fainting in choruses, to the needy bird,
The keen destroyer, chaunting his war-song.

Triumphant lightning danced upon his rims,
Withered with angers; and his shadow fell—
Then gloomy grew the Titan's face and cold,
Before the tremor of such quenchless wrath.
Its pale crest sank, its fierce pipe swelled no more
But in his bowels, through a sea of blood
(Like the dark conflict of opposing sails
Which in the midnight storms do sink and drown,
Blown bubbles fading in a watery world)
Sank its curved beak, until his body yawned
Deadly and wide, a ghast and sobbing wound.
Then brawled his blood along the frigid stones,
The hoar biters, jagged with spiteful brows,
Until its gush rained on the misty spires,
The cold gray rocks, that snored i' the winds below;
Dim giants nodding to the frozen sweep
Of boundless ages; the grim dowagers
Out of all time—its hard, griping beak
Draggled and tore, till, with plundering wrath,
It gorged; returning with each cavernous delve
To tireless slaughter; the long shreds trailed
Ruinously, while his liver bitten through,
Rolled on the crags—and the strong Titan swooned.

*   *   *   *   *   *

Out from the clouds now swelled a joyous song,
And Jove looked down to mock the prophet sage;
His giddy rout quick tending to his will—
Resplendent slaves, a vast and radiant throng:
Over their heads lost in a span of gold,
A bright arch glowed in myriad-show'ring stars.
"And this," quoth Jove, "is the great god of Man,
Who filched our fires, and like a guilty thief,
Sped with our darts from Vulcan's torrid forge?
The same, bestowed upon a race of fools,
With which I thrashed black Typhon to the earth
And crushed the monster with a hundred hills;
The Typhon, whose red rage doth seethe and broil
In hell tumultuous, and whose heart-groan quakes
Hard-lingering thunders from Mount Ætna's womb;—
And there he'll gasp and roar eternally,
Buried and damned in frenzy-gulfing fires
Hissing and whitening—Hades withers him,
And its harsh tongue chafes him with blistering flames.
And such for thee the fate I will reserve,
And in thy fate enclose the race of Man."
Prometheus looked not, for his face was dead;
And the earth-light fluttered o'er his glazéd eyes,
Throwing its random shade and useless gleam

In sick reflection of thought's varying blaze—
Like to the beauty of the vacant mind
Masking reality, aye, where stirring souls,
Worn travelers 'mid the lonely crowds around,
Pass grieving on, with eyes averted low,
Nor once confront the gen'ral stare of death.
Prometheus dreamed; nor long the deathly swoon
Bound his great limbs—its vast and sudden thrall
Lifted like darkness to the sun's bright pulse,
Paling the shadows of the drowsy world,
And morning danced along his wakening veins.
Yet not in vain each agonizing dart
Stings the rough wound, or sends the reeling brain
Down to the darkest gulf of deep'ning swoon;
Pain is the lamp of Death's refulgent mine;
The death of body is the life of soul;
And everything brings forth a just reward—
Aye, from the darkest hell shall Genius mount
Ere heaven be gained and sternest Truth be won.
Prometheus gazed; but 'twas a faster life
That thrilled in his quick veins—a life new born
From pain—and Time shall yet its bliss prolong:*
His blood ran surging from the living lyre,
Thrilling his nerves in a long rain of fire;
In joyant frenzy the first song began,
With burst ecstatic—'twas the Song of Man.

  * * * * * *

" Ill-reaching Jove! thou rotten sheath of pride,
Whom fawning slaves have perched above our thrones;
Thou stool-grown emanation of a night,
Poor bubble quiring to the wanton winds,
Stretching with empty greatness to thy death:
Thou, whom to parley with offends me more
Than to grow drunken in the lewd embrace
And leprous kissings of a bloated hag,
Drummed with hoarse music from the lazy town,
The common gangway of the reechy horde,
Rolled, with the fevers, from each foreign sail,
Till worn Dishonor spews upon her name,
And forty years, confessed, she stands a whore:
Thou vaunter, though my weaker nerves do groan,
And my stiff heart cries forth this heinous crime;
Yet to thy face I dash contemptuous scorn,
And tell thee thou'rt contemned, confined, abridged;
That here, within these limbs, a Titan reigns,
Nor all Jove's spleen commands this trenchéd land.

---

* Knowledge is the foe of pain. *To know is to not suffer.* This refers to all pain. *There is no pain but ignorance; there is no crime but ignorance.*

Oh, 'tis a joy that prophet bards will know
To point the strong, and ban them in the tide,
And burst triumphant of quick-verging pow'r;
To gaze with silent scorn upon the fool,
As down he wanders, clattering unto death:
And thus for thee, vaunt semblance of a god,
Grown giddy in that rabblement's applause,
The glozing train which frets the tainted air
With strumpet phrases—ye shall tend me now,
Dull beggars craving from the prophet's store,
While fear sits crownéd on your ashen brows—
Rend me with flames, rain earthquakes on my head,
My voice would eat you through a world of steel,
(E'en though a whisper knocked upon its walls)
Hard in the silent strength of swerveless truth.
Laugh while ye may—thus do I prophecy
Men shall be kings, but royal Jove shall die.

*　　*　　*　　*　　*　　*

Turn thy stern brows upon these gloomy wastes,
Where cold winds mutter through the sobbing mists,
Swishing lone horror through the frozen blood
Of that wild king, the conqueror of gods—
With quaking bones he cow'rs upon the ground,
A shagged outcast ; wearied and out-run
By the moaning bear, monstrous, rude, and stark
With railing murder ; the hoarse plunderer,
The slow blood-hound, with the huge swinging head
Bitterly gasping ;
Frighting the hills with his rough cloud of hair,
Till ravaged Nature cries upon his rush,
And tracks his roars with loudly-crashing pines—
Against this cloud behold faint man arise,
Fierce with despair, staring the dark approach
Silent and awful ; then twangs th' unsteady air
With roaring peals, whose soughing strain resounds
Throughout the vast cathedral of the wilds,
A thousand echoes chanting—
Leaps the stone-point high-cheering thro' the air
Man's war-dint glorious ; comet of the brave,
The death-portending spear—rends the rough claws
Tugging his hair ; then with his ragged arm
Drownéd in mingling streams all gashed and torn,
He darkly closes 'gainst the monstrous hill,
With mountainous war-songs thrilling.
And, aye, that shout will shake the gods on high,
Rabid with hate and wild with pale despair.
Then shall the bear lament with reeling groans
The biting menace of the windy spear

As down he roars, stunned in the blast of death.
Where sinks his foe—the monarch of the world.

* * * * * *

Behold the Scythians rise, a host of bards
Stretching from Inde ; the ravens heralding
God's chosen bands, the grand philosophers,
Terrific in tunes. In their midst I hear
Emmania's* gathering songs, lost i' the tongues ;
And by their sides the Saxon voice is heard,
Tuning their war-blades ;
The Saxon, from whose heart-strings shall be made
The clairseach bright (the emblem of Ierne,
Sad Erin of the Sorrows), the great harp
That floats triumphant o'er the convex globe,
Drowning the jar of multitudinous strains.
All this fades quickly in dissolving dreams,
Whiles chronic Time moves dimly in the view ;
Hobbling to some, to others charging on,
Slow to the quick and hasty to the slow ;
The coward, sage, fool, poet, boy and man,
Have each their varying estimate of time.

* * * * * *

The nations cry, the light swims in the air,
And Homer smiles, the foremost of the rude,
Ragged and blind.   The first of all the grand
Roams through the world to beg a little bread.
Alas ! the world makes beggars of its kings,
Spurning the greatest, on whose brain it feeds ;
Then call the poets proud, wry-mouthed, harsh,
If they return its justice on the world !
The world is *wrong*, for *mind* alone can tell,
And Genius *right* in heaven, earth or hell.

* * * * * *

Swells the grand chorus ! Lo, Æschylus comes,
Stormy in tragedies, and in his train
Greece lifts her brows and shakes the trump of Time.
With fearful note she stuns the freighted years
Resounding thro' the golden seas of Morn—
And to that blast a million trumps shall blow,
Bright'ning the views with burning pomp sublime,
While swim the ages on resplendent sails,
Hailing the suns of dim futurities—
Rome trembles—and the victor shouts arise
O'er helms ablaze on wide Pharsalia's field,
And Cæsar nods upon the sweating spears,
While reeks the vapors of a broiling host,

---

*Emmania, a palace in Ulster, existing before the days of Malachy.

Choked in the dust and dry with deeds of rage.
Yet from that field soft Lucian's star shall glow,
To burn triumphant o'er great Pompey's fall.
Aye shall the bard proclaim his verse the age,
For nations die without a voice in song;
The man may speak, the *nation* cries in tunes—
And paltry times are beggars of the dead,
Propped by the scornful bones of nobler men.
Such be the days between the Grecian's fall
And Cæsar's rise—but in the dazzling sun
Of Rome's wide splendor bards go forth renowned,
Shaking their locks with joyant majesty,
A royal throng with Virgil at their head;
Greater by reason of the coming night,
That spreads foul darkness o'er the groping world;
Through whose lone waste shall Dante tune in tears,
Blind, on the threshold of the living times.
The next I see from all the countries round,
From sunny Spain and fruitful Portugal,
Nay, from the borders of the icy lands
One vast aurora tending—Wisdom sings,
And haggard Ignorance shrinks dumbly down,
To dash its head against the crags of hell—
Grief dries the breast of that most aged whore,
Spawner of fools, the foul and withered hag,
Green-visaged, spleenful, swinish, brown and rough,
Whose bitter face will churn the galls of men
With retching throbs; whose spider charms no more
Shall guile the love-born with a veil of gauze—
Knowledge has bound her, and its harshest knell
Eats like hot poison through her blasted ears,
Intolerable tortures sounding.
Now comes the rounded semblance of the globe
With the vast brows; his eyes, harmonious seas
Wherein the visual breezes of the world
Blow ceaseless melodies, and Shakspeare waves,
Lord of his times, thrice-crowned by God Itself.
Nations will hail the illustrious joy-maker
With cheers interminable; India swells,
Dashing its thunders from the Eastern heights
To Erin of the Streams; over the main,
Beyond the storm-ways of the blust'ring surge,
Shall sound the chaunt o' the bard victorious;
Over the land of Poe, whose starry flame
Shall dance triumphant o'er the western sphere,
Lighting the poles—lord of the bursting brine.

\   *   *   *   *   *   *

Still greater bards arise, a dauntless throng,
The dread world-scorners, fainting with fierce love

And rage uproarious; their hearts resound,
And their thrilling hair, like pattering rain,
Show'ring in chills, o'er faces stark with joy.—
Well shall the world have reason to rejoice
O'er truths that stir the frenzies of its bards;
Death-striking thrills, torn from the poet's ribs,
And whirled aloft, e'en from his burning brain,
To spread new light upon the toiling race,
In whose grand love the minstrel finds reward.
And some for love shall lift the pond'rous globe,
Bursting with deadly sobs, and to the strain
Swoon as they cry, " I have not lived in vain."

*   *   *   *   *   *

Now shines the sunlight on a golden time,
And all are bards; the earth is drowned in rays;
From noon to noon the sun of mind sweeps on,
Intolerable splendor streaming —
And to this day our morn shall be as night,
Our greatest but a dark barbarian. —
Scarce from the womb shall prophet-bards arise,
Bright with the knowledge of high-soaring minds,
To converse by the parallax of stars — *
Piercing the laws until the past illumes,
And every hour confronts his blazing stare —
"On such a day was this, or that, performed,
And such the faces of my groping sires" —
Till the mute passion of the fadeless past
Tells its own tale of deathless souls beyond."

*   *   *   *   *   *

Prometheus ceased, and laughed unto the skies,
While his vast ribs swelled outwards to his roars,
And the glad hills rolled answer to each peal
In jocund echoes bounding.   The streams danced,
And the hoarse caves shook back their bass profound;
All earth rejoiced the downfall of the gods,
Pale ghosts declining to the rising sun
Which turned the mists into a rosy sea,
Washing the crags with deepest crimson fire,
Till Euxine flamed — And, o'er the smiling haze,
Prometheus slept amidst the golden rays.

---

*Ignorance, or a low state of mentality, gives us a false idea of distance. Thus, if we could hear, see, and smell sufficiently, we could mentally exist *in* the moon at the distance of two hundred and forty thousand miles. Hence, knowledge always gives one a greater sweep of vision, which originates that which is called the sublime.

ETIQUETTE FOR YOUNG LADIES.

By Mr. Downey Gabb, late Professor of Deportment at Blushington Hall.

The object of the following paragraphs is, not to supply what is found in the vulgar books of etiquette, but rather to finish where they have left off; giving completion to the character and a tone to the behavior; making, in fact, a lady *by rote*, above all criticism and "low form."

It is considered among the *best* circles that the use of the letter R is vulgar — pray avoid it, as nobody but over-earnest people use it at all. One thing you must recollect: that, though some would say the omission of this single letter shows a weakness *somewhere* in the individual, yet you must also bear in mind that, as society is composed of people whose breeding gives them but little chance to be individual, the less individuality you possess the more likely you are to rise in society.

Keep a scrap book for poetry. Do not paste anything in it, however, but newspaper sentiment. No poetry is good that displays fervidness — a genteel and dreamy zephyr wherein a commonplace riddle is deftly shoved is quite *haut ton* at present. Mere poetry with a meaning is unfashionable. It has been said that poetry is comprehensible only to poets, and that as there is but one (perhaps unknown) in a million, the only way in which the cultured can hope to excel these vulgar Bohemians is to confuse our judgments with woven fancies of legerdemain.

When a gentleman is admiring the contour of your face, do not turn away, but bite your lips to make them look red. Nobody understands the trick, and it may pass for a pretty bit of impatient modesty.

In painting the face, leave all but your cheeks as white and thick as possible. The rouge on the cheeks must be blended off, otherwise they may think you are related to the pantomime people. Ladies with white hair look best when painted. (Mem.—Gentlemen do not see paint. Nobody but your own dearest friends are ever aware of its existence, and even then its visibility depends on *your* belief. Faith removes mountains.)

Cultivate the acquaintance of artists and musical *virtuosi*. The artists must be painters of chinaware and lovers of bric-a-brac only. You will know a *virtuoso* when you see him by his thick lips and dirty hair. (Mem.—Nobody but foreigners with broken English to be tolerated.)

In speaking at a party, it is considered *recherche* to use a few words of French now and then. Cavillers will say that it betokens a shallow spirit; but, to my thinking, it is both polished and refined. Do not, however, use too much, as it may bewilder the *societaires*, and you must not expose them to needless alarm. "*Apropos*" and *"n' importe"* can be frequently used and *"blasé"* sounds well. But you must always be careful of your depth, and trench not upon the ignorance of the guests, for are they not one with you in heart and soul ? In your walks or shopping, you must turn around and stare at every new dress you see. When a lone looking widow passes by with a faded hat, it is allowable to smirk and giggle, for giggling betokens the superiority of your position, and it is well these sullen things should know it!

When a remark is passed that may be too deep for present comprehension, look to the quarter from which it came, and if the person who uttered it is common-looking in his dress, smile at it and shake your head; for were wisdom to be the rule, the enjoyments of society would be blotted out in an instant. Therefore giggle and turn away from the speaker.

In entering a street-car, fatigued, after a quarter of an hour's shopping, do not stare at the gentlemen if you desire a seat, but look towards the laborer, as he is oftenest the most chivalrous. Of course, he is tired, but thanks are unnecessary. It is your right, for are you not a *lady?*

If you are doubtful of your ancestry, it is considered the best course to originate one. Puritan is the best at present. Of course, the Puritans were but a poor set of rogues, but then nobody knows, and the name sounds well, if the features are round and foreign.

When visiting a picture gallery, talk very loud in praise of the dimmer Old Masters and go into raptures, *after you are sure of the name.* (Mem.—Millet, Corot, and other unnaturalists are at present in vogue.) Criticise the smaller defects of Dore. True art is not expressed in unutterable grandeur or pathos. The "Shepherd's Chief Mourner" is defective in a few points—the nails in the coffin are a trifle too dark, or at least a trifle too light. (Mem.—Say "*chiaroscuro*" every now and then.)

When asked concerning literature, confess ignorance of Shakspeare's, Byron's or Dickens' works; but you must know all of the monthly magazine writers; for are they not fashionable? (Mem.—Howells and Henry James, thought shallow and dawdling by the merely reflective set, are the geniuses of *the hour*.)

Nobody can be a true lady unless she has been to Europe. The sight of some streets rattled through, by night mostly, some mountains from out of a carriage window, some lousy lazzaroni, "St. Peters, you know," and the "Crystal Palace," gives wide experience to the shallowest mind and furnishes subject for thought that lasts even beyond recollection. Travel enlarges the sympathies, and tones in a few months the saturated vulgarity pre-natally inherited.

Now, while it is *de rigeur* at present to doubt somewhat of the inspiration of Scriptures, yet it is not considered good-breeding to omit the periodic visit to the fortune teller. He would be wise indeed who could afford to do without them. They are well worth ten dollars a visit!

It is very wrong, nay, more than that, it is *unbecoming* to hint about what the eccentric and unfashionable denominate as "Womans Rights." Such uncomfortable subjects would turn society away from the path of ease and indifference and ban the little *bagatelles* that make up our existence; nay, it would even be an excuse for some ladies to rise above us and encourage mind to the detriment of all exclusion and deportment. Of course, there are a few uncomfortable bodies who, dissatisfied with the conservative element (the truest in our natures), would seek to exalt woman above what they would call the silly and sick-minded gravities of fashion, placing her as far as nature allows, on the level of exact equality with man. But these are only *crazy* people, who cannot see the perfection that lies beneath the laws and usances of society. Ladies may act and look scorn upon men as superiors; but it is highly improper to hint about the fact of equality—nobody but low people do it.

When a person is invited to your house (an artist or a musician), if he be of the poorer orders, send him, after he has entertained you for a few hours, to supper with the servants. Sometimes, these people ignorant of good-breeding, with a forgetful effusiveness, may hold out their hands at parting; extend but two fingers, as that is the *only way* you possess of showing your superiority.

A selfish, money-loving, or hypocritical disposition, though a trifle unsuitable at times, must not, however, prevent one from owning a pew wherein to display their finery. It is considered unfashionable to attend any of those churches in which ministers deliver the tenets they are paid for delivering. Earnestness wearies one, and orthodox notions are a trifle *passé*. Go, instead, to the spicier churches where the sermon is composed of political gossip and events of the day; you will get the name of being religious; besides, it will save you the trouble of reading those tiresome newspapers. In the drawing-room you must speak of your minister as "our dear pastor." What if the most popular be charged with adultery and other peccadilloes; we are but human after all!

Above all things remember that you were "put" on this earth to look after *yourself* alone. You cannot do better than to lace yourself as tight as Bridget's arm can strain; it will shrink your interior, destroy your digestion, and give you the delicate look which all who are not diseased prize so highly. (Mem.—Vinegar is recommended, as it weakens the blood.)

No cosmetic is of any account until it has been pronounced dangerous. The rule is the same as that which we apply to medicine; which is held to be useless until it is too nauseating to taste. Arsenic makes a complexion as white as snow, and, in time, gives a beautiful *hectic* flush to the cheeks. (Mem.—Do not be afraid to use it in large quantities, for it is estimated that a horse can stand it for at least sixteen weeks.)

All young ladies should possess a chaperone. Some will say that a chaperone is but the needing of an old harlot for the schooling of a young one, and that the restraint imposed but adds to the secret pleasures of intrigue—but this is only the talk of mere thinkers and reasoners, people who are altogether out of the pale of society. Some of the *élite*, from their way of seeing things, would imagine that ladies who need so much watching, are, though insolent and contemptible, less virtuous than the poorer sisters over whom they affect superior airs; but this is refuted on the ground that so very few of our highest ladies marry for anything else beside money.

It is considered the height of impropriety to read from a book of science, particularly the sciences of embryology or anatomy. It is immodest to pretend a knowledge of the structure that Nature has given you. It will be time enough when you are married; then you can consult Mrs. Hagge, the intellectual midwife. From that person you will find that your lungs are situated behind your ears, and that a child with a caul on is going to be President of the United States. Experience alone must teach you. The men may understand all about that which they never feel, however. When you are broken down and rendered helpless from want of kuowledge, you may then take up a book on physiology and nobody will notice it. (Mem.—You must not under any condition inform your children, however; let them find it out as you have done, else half the romance of lust would be taken away, and they might marry for true companionship, or, what the vulgar style, love.)

Train up your daughters to fascinate alone. It is unnecessary to teach them the art of enforcing respect after the honey-moon is over; it is enough that they be married. Once off your hands they may go to the devil. Let them cry as much as they like over the secret fact that John or Thomas seeks sensible enjoyment elsewhere. Instead of educating them to enter into man's intellectual soul, let them be instructed in piano fingering, giggling, waltzing, etc., etc.—men will come, idealize, grow intoxicated by the excitement around, marry, and——vent their regard over a club newspaper.

Always be kind to the poor and distressed. The best way to do this is to attend a charity ball, where you get the worth of your money and act the patron at the same time. Visit the jails. Your attention, however, must not be directed to the impoverished and innocent man, but to the low-browed murderer, whose cell you must deck with flowers, sending him an occasional *billet-doux*, to comfort his sensitive heart.

When you are at a watering-place, six dresses a day must be worn. It shows that your life-idea centers in dress, and enhances your charms in the eyes of the thoughtful few. Some would hint that there are beggars who would refuse your hand with a Roman's scorn, pretending that mind alone is the true patent of nobility ; but were this the case, mankind would have seen it long ago and have elevated mind instead of condition and money. No ! society is not *barbarian* as this would seem to hint, nor do we know of any too contemptuous in mind to care to rise in it. Society cannot be *barbarian*, for it is not sustained by imbecile minds, nor does it exclude all that is deep, high-minded, progressive and true.

THE PALE ROSE OF ERIN.

1884.

I swept upon a burning chord, and to my love I struck the lyre,
She's the pale rose of Erin, high, majestic, pure and beauteous;
Her breasts are like the tender snows that flush the rosy morning's fire,
And ah! upon the melting strings my rippling praise shall ne'er expire,
But weep in smiles the merry name of Kathaleen ni Houlahan,—
The gentle, soft and merry name of Kathaleen ni Houlahan.

No Stranger of the Dismal Tongue can hope to cheer or pleasure you;
The trading horde will soon return; no clown shall e'er enjoy thee;
The Saxon dames are pale with fear, in vain they strove to measure you;
With modest eyne and saintly brows—the ringing bards will treasure you
Until the breeze is sick with love of Kathaleen ni Houlahan—
And faints to bear the liquid song of Kathaleen ni Houlahan.

Her beauty fans my heart with tunes, her eyes are deeper than the stars
When dimly sinks the golden moon to slumber in the surges—
But now she sleeps in Brasil's Isle, remote from strife and foreign jars;
She tends upon the prophet bard and wakes upon the rise of Mars;
While Grannia smiles, and nods the name of Kathaleen ni Houlahan—
Old Grannia smiles and times the name of Kathaleen ni Houlahan.

She is my pulse, my living blood, my rest, my gentle pillow;
All other maids I do disown, she is my dream of morning;
No more I'll swell the nightly tune beneath the mournful willow—
The birds are whistling to the tones I've show'r'd across the billow,
And aye the birds will chirp the song of Kathaleen ni Houlahan—
Forget their varied notes to sing of Kathaleen ni Houlahan.

From want of time and space, the writer has been compelled to withhold his humorous writings, which are pronounced the best by his friends, and his war-sagas, the latter a series of savage, abbreviated and *unmodern* chaunts, wild with lamentation and rejoicing—a grim collection, harsh and riotous, in which art explodes, unable to confine the naked energies of uproarious nature. Poetry in Irish means *a fiery dart;* such was the poetry of our skalds and bards; the bard must *feel* more in order to express more, and in the horrible tempests of feeling that sweep the spirit of the open mind, I behold God's letters-patent, the passport of the bards. In vain the cold miser attunes himself; the lean cur who would skin a bug, or suck a dying pauper's blood for gain—he is wedded to his own gripe, and never feels the fires of " sacred invention." Nothing but pure invention is poetry.

THE DYING CONVICT'S LAMENT.

May, 1884.

Tune—"*Erin, my Country, I Love thy Green Bowers.*

No more through the vales with my *clairsech* I'll wander,
    In chains I lament thee, sweet Erin *a-ruin;*
While fade the dark walls through my tears, as I ponder;
    For oh, to my grief, my poor heart's in the mould!
No more shall I voice to the heart-shaking sallies,
That wake the glad hills where the lone trumpet rallies;
Or bend o'er my love through the mist-weaving valleys;
    Alas, I must weep in the jail of Clonmel.

When lovers return in the shade of the bushes.
    Kind Erin mavournyeen, sweet Erin *a-ruin;*
I sigh for the times when I plucked the green rushes;
    But oh, to my grief, my poor heart's in the mould!
No more through the fields will I greet the soft showers,
Where sun-waving Morn flings its mist o'er the bowers,
Or watch the red throats warbling sweet o'er the flowers;
    Alas, I must weep in the jail of Clonmel.

To think—oh, my sorrow; the hot tears will blind me!—
    The cold stone awaits me, sweet Erin a-ruin;
When bowed with white age that the Saxon would bind me;
    Ma vrone to my fortunes, my heart's in the mould!
I've braved the dark storm 'neath the low, ruined rafter,
The hoar blight—O God!—when the plague followed after;
Then homeless I wept, thro' the hoarse winter's laughter—
    To sink dead and cold in the jail of Clonmel!

Though traitors declaim, 'tis my heart's only token,
    And dear to my soul is the comfort I draw,
No traitor lies dead when my lonely heart's broken—
    Sound the grand *slainté go! Slan leat go bragh!*
Nor grieve that I struck with a manly endeavor;
From Erin no Saxon my heart-strings can sever,
Though chills the worn heart that lies silent forever,
    To sleep with his chains in the jail of Clonmel.

LAMENT FOR CAPTAIN JAMES SADLER

And one hundred and thirty of his passengers and crew, who went down on the night of April 18th in the steamer "State of Florida," which foundered in a collision with the "Pomona" (the latter sinking at the first shock), in mid-ocean.

Tune—Original.

My dreams are sad and I wake in tears —
The days have changed yet no friend appears;
For gentle Sadler I deeply mourn,
And the loss of those who will ne'er return.

Ne'er suits the pride of the pampered crew
Who spurn the hand of the jacket blue,
To brave the storms of the cloudy main,
Where mountains roar and horrid lightnings rain.

'Tis scarce six weeks since the western tide
Did slant her decks for the shores of Clyde —
With shrouded pinions she left the shore,
On the dark Atlantic to sail no more.

On moon-lit waves I have heard the bells
That Time's alarm to the seamen tells;
On heaving decks I have roamed the sea,
For to man the shrouds was my destiny.

The night was drear and the ocean dim,
When that blood-light chased the darkness grim;
Hoarse thunders crashed 'neath the scowling gleam,
And in smothered cries sank its fatal beam.

O Christ we drown! and the watch espied,
Where swung the lights o'er the dashing side,
A frightful wound where the howling brine
With its raging tons swept the stokers' mine.

What fearful sights met the rising swarm!
While railed the gong with a dread alarm —
With calling frenzies the ropes were low'red,
And the first boat plunged where the darkness roared

The vast hull reared as she tore the seas,
And ploughed a dirge thro' the mournful breeze —
With terror dumb by the launch they stood,
For the vessel *stormed* o'er the briny flood.

The funnels groaned, and they sought in vain
To float their launch on the hissing main ;
To stem the seas and his *grave* to clear
The valves were fastened by the engineer.

We're lost, all lost ! to return he tried,
Where sank the rails in the yawning tide ;
'Mid rumbling waters he searched the gloom—
And his cries were lost in that iron tomb.

With bounding speed, then, the big ship soared,
And struck the launch that swept over-board ;
A frozen call sighed upon the lee,
And its echoes died on that raving sea.

With bubbling laughter and moanings wild,
The mother shrieked 'neath her drowning child ;
While fitful tones swelled above the crowds
Who cried with horror on the whistling shrouds.

With dreadful sounds now they dinned the air
And rent the skies with their black despair—
While some, more stern, moaned with hopes wrung down.
"Is *this* my fate, O, God ? to sink and drown "!

That night, unseen, where the ocean wailed,
The strongest wept as the waves prevailed,
And mourned their fate that they ne'er would see
The sweet home faces in High Germanie.

O God, make haste ! and the screamers toll,
The stern-lights fade where the corpses roll—
The boatmen cried as that captain brave,
Sank like a hero in the gloomy wave.

Cried Sadler, "Messmates, my duty's done ;
In full command, now, my glass is run—"
He waved his hand as he rang the bell,
And the ship went down to his last farewell.

I've cast my fate with that seaman true,
When flame and smoke o'er his vessel flew;
Ne'er base and low, did he earn disgrace,
Nor shame the remnant of the sea-king race.

Mourn, seamen, mourn for that hero's end !
And weep ye brave for the sailors' friend !
The winds are drear, and the tempest raves
Where his body drowns 'neath the lonely waves.

SCIENTIFIC ADDENDA.

I have had years to think of what I have expounded in the "Mathematic," and isolated facts have been grouped into harmonious wholes. Space is *first cause* for infinite or *all* space means inextension. *All*-space, in itself, is causeless or uncaused, for a thing *must* be extended or not extended, and space is *both!* The *first cause* of everything, the uncaused, is *now* comprehensible, and we need not refer to a second cause as handier and more convenient to the mind. Man's next great flight lies in the domain of prophecy; to foresee combinations of thought. Look to your future bards, mark what I pen, for they are your kings and prophets—they are to be known as scorners of ignorance; haters of misers and cowards; unblemished by artificiality; devoid of the bitter blood of merchants; tramplers of curs and lamenters of the poor. Rome has decayed, and chivalry has begun.

Time is distance, and distance is nothing but time. Time and *space* are one. The past is *in reality* distant from us, for the world is moving. *Time is successive* and cannot occupy the same space—no two times exist at once. To deny that time is distance is to abolish fact—to abolish fact is simply to merge all fact into a principle that annihilates itself back again to the same facts, we alone changing; simply because we have viewed a thing on both sides.

There is no such thing as spirit—Spiritualism has no foundation. What may pass muster as spirit is refined matter. Spiritualism however is nothing but the dregs of hashed-up Christianity, with errors old enough to be stinking. Those who have passed beyond are separated from this world by distance and sympathy—we are but maggots to them, and could not understand *one idea* they would wish to convey. The world is not receptive even to its philosophers; how then could fools understand the foreign sympathy of so-called death? Depend upon it that *mind alone* can be receptive to them, a mind that by superhuman sorrow and transcendent sensitiveness has absolutely had greatness enough to *cry from the soul* for truth, truth *not* of this world—to one, inspired, who had outgrown *all* ephemeral sympathies—to such, the past will touch, with the whispered sentences of unknown truth.

Decay is caused by reflection. The reason *why* a void is force, is that its center being a pure solid, or point of explosion, rejects the encroachments of the exterior universe. All things decay most that reflect light—darkness and light themselves are *almost* totally undecayable. Light being nothing but *darkness in motion*, the whole question of light is settled—it is nothing but *trembling space;* not *air*, mind you, but the pure, elastic, densified ideal. As space never ceases to move after being once agitated, it follows that light never decreases, for it can combine only into color and intelligence.